Angel
Letters

Angel
Letters

Sophy Burnham

BALLANTINE BOOKS

NEW YORK

Library of Congress Cataloging-in-Publication Data
Angel letters / [compiled by] Sophy Burnham.—1st ed.
p.   cm.
Companion vol. to: A book of angels / Sophy Burnham. c1990.
ISBN 0-345-37342-1
1. Burnham, Sophy. Book of angels. 2. Angels. I. Burnham,
Sophy. II. Burnham, Sophy. Book of angels.
BL477.B88   1991
291.2' 15—dc20   91-91880
                                                                CIP

Text design by Beth Tondreau Design
Manufactured in the United States of America
First Edition: September 1991
10 9 8 7 6 5 4 3 2 1

I wish to thank all those who so generously responded to A Book of Angels. *I apologize to the many people whose stories, for lack of space, cannot be used here.*

This is your book, dedicated to you and your angels.

Giotto. Angel
from the
Arena Chapel.

· INTRODUCTION ·

Angel letters. We send letters to our angels. And letters come back to us, like leaves floating on the air. They land on the pond of our consciousness so softly sometimes we hardly feel them, and only by the ripples growing outward in ever-larger concentric circles do we recognize their presence, see the fallen leaf.

This book, the sequel to *A Book of Angels*, consists of a small selection of the many letters written in response to that earlier work.

The letters, an outpouring of personal experiences and spiritual confessions, started arriving as soon as the book was published. I filed them by subject—angel stories, car accidents, dreams, spirits and ghosts, visions, voices, and other mysteries touching on the divine. There were requests to meet, requests for more information, requests for me to speak or hold seminars on angels. Readers asked how they could get in touch with, work with, befriend these healing guides.

So beloved are angels that people sent books, poems, pamphlets, drawings, photos, slides of angel paintings, postcards, music tapes, and works of art; almost all expressed the most moving gratitude for publication of *A Book of Angels*:

I want to tell you how grateful I am for your beautiful book. Right from the beginning it gripped me as no book has and sent chills up my spine . . . nothing short of a miracle for me.

I have only gotten to page 57 of your book, when I knew that I had to write you.

I have just finished reading your *A Book of Angels* and knew even before the end that I was to write to you. I would like to tell you what a wonderful gift you have given to the world.

I recently bought your book. . . . Though I have thus far only read up to the third chapter, which has already at certain points brought me to tears, I feel overwhelmingly compelled to write you.

One young woman wrote that her mother had been reading the book aloud to her at the fireplace. Another said that it was on the bedside table of a dying friend.

Again and again people wrote that they were "drawn to" the book. One woman was driving in her car, troubled and disconsolate, when she saw a bookstore and had the sudden urge to stop. Another felt the book "jump off the shelf" at her. Other letters came telling of experiences with angels or rapture or ecstasy, with light, or God, however that word is understood.

We *all* have angels guiding, guarding us; that's what

these letters show—the marks of angels in the sand. They stand as fragile signatures, indicating that something stepped there for a moment and passed on, and we see them only briefly, like footprints before the tide comes in and washes clean the sand. Angels everywhere. What will bring their help? Asking. Giving thanks. Who will recognize them? Anyone. Or no one possibly.

They come to children, to people of great brilliance, to madmen, to those of deep simplicity and purity of heart. They come more easily to ordinary people than to those preoccupied with worldly power.

Since finishing *A Book of Angels* I have come to a personal belief: that we live surrounded by ghosts, by spirits, not only in our imagination, as metaphors of our past, but also in reality—our departed loved ones watching us—and we are also surrounded by superior spiritual beings of great light and magnificence, manifestations of the divine, who want for us poor humans better things than we can possibly imagine. And I believe that if we leave them alone and present ourselves, like children, in total trust and love and humble gratitude, then they will pour their blessings on us overwhelmingly. They play with us. They look after us. They heal us, touch us, comfort us with invisible warm hands, and always they try to give us what we want.

Scientifically they cannot be seen, but then neither can a black hole in space. Still, their presence is known, and

Stone walls do not a prison make,
Nor iron bars a cage;
Minds innocent and quiet take
That for an hermitage;
If I have freedom in my love
And in my soul am free,
Angels alone that soar above
Enjoy such liberty.
—RICHARD LOVELACE
"To Althea: From Prison"

. . . .

perhaps the letters in this little volume will serve to remind you of moments when you, too, have felt an angel's touch or heard the whisper of a wing or received a missive invisibly floating past, to say, "We're here," and "Don't forget."

· AUTHOR'S NOTE ·

The writers of these letters have generously given permission to use their stories and full names. Five of the writers, however, requested anonymity to protect their privacy, and this I have tried to respect using the statement: "Name Withheld By Request."

I have used only the initials of one writer to protect the identity of those about whom she speaks.

SB

Angel
Letters

Edmund Dulac. Frontispiece
from *The Love of a Foolish Angel.*

he following incident occurred in 1958 when I was a navy jet-fighter pilot. Our aircraft carrier was steaming in a northerly direction in the Pacific Ocean, east of the Sea of Japan, one late fall day. Farther to the east a typhoon was moving north as well. The seas were heavy but not too rough to prevent air operations. Our flight, the last one for the day, launched around three P.M. and lasted for an uneventful hour and a half.

When we returned, however, we found the ship pitching up and down and rolling in such heavy seas that our planes had great difficulty landing, either because of the uneven deck or because the plane ahead was fouled up in the arresting gear, blocking the landing area. Six times I tried to land and six times was waved off. I became anxious. Each landing approach consumed 150 to 200 pounds of fuel (a pound is about 7 gallons of jet fuel). I was down to 450 pounds of fuel.

On my eighth attempt I was again waved off.

"What is your fuel state?" the Air Boss asked by radio.

"One hundred fifty pounds." The Air Boss asked for my intentions. I could either climb to parachute altitude and eject before I ran out of fuel or make one more attempt to land, with no chance of parachute escape, but if I failed, the plane would go into the sea. It was by now

He shall give his angels charge over thee
to keep thee in all thy ways.
They shall bear thee up in their hands,
lest thou dash thy foot against a stone.

PSALMS 91:11–12

· · · ·

Any man who does not believe in miracles in not a realist.
—DAVID BEN-GURION

• • • •

early evening and the ship was laboring in seas so rough that the rescue helicopter had landed. My plane was the last one in the air. I decided that my chances for survival after parachuting into a cold, mountainous sea with night approaching were nonexistent. Even in calm conditions a water landing was not advised, as the aircraft was known to blow apart on water entry. I told the Air Boss that I would make one last attempt.

As I flew downwind and prepared to turn onto the base leg of my approach, I prayed out loud into my oxygen mask but not over the radio: "Lord Jesus Christ, I need your help now or I will die. This is beyond my ability to control." My wife of six months was expecting our first child. I prayed, "I want a family. I want to see my children. But if it is your will that I should die now, then I accept your will. I will fly this plane to the best of my abilities until the end." I turned onto my approach heading. Suddenly a feeling of great warmth, love, and indescribable joy overcame me. My anxiety was gone. Although my hands were on the controls, a far better pilot than me was flying the plane. I knew instantly my prayer was being answered and that I had nothing to fear. As the plane let down to the carrier from a distance of about two miles and an altitude of about 1,000 feet, I looked at the ship in utter amazement. It appeared to be floating on top of a huge upwelling of water. The waves were not penetrating the upwelling and the ship was floating level as in a calm sea. This lasted for some twenty to twenty-five seconds. Just as the tail hook engaged the arresting wire, the divine assistance ceased and the ship heeled sharply to starboard. But I was safely aboard. The aircraft line chief told me later that my aircraft was bone dry of jet fuel when checked before refueling.

Incidentally I did not tell my experience to my squadron mates; and the ship personnel were not in a position to see the upwelling, which, as I recall, extended no more than twenty yards on either side of the ship. As you can imagine, I was overwhelmed by the incident, and twenty-five-year-old fighter pilots don't preach to their squadron mates. But I knew what had happened!

This contact with the Supreme Being affected my life. It made human goals of wealth and control and position seem of little consequence. It's made me very uneasy in the presence of unprincipled men and women, even to the point of feeling chills.

Since then I have turned my life over to Christ. I have had a wonderful marriage of thirty-three years, children and grandchildren, and been able to retire from business at the age of fifty-eight after the usual ups and downs.

Odd that people will trust their savings in the hands of a banker or investment broker but not think to put their happiness in the hands of God.

Name withheld by request

· · · · · · · · · · · · · · · · · · · ·

Many of the letters tell of lost items being recovered or of receiving unexpected gifts, such as a pair of gloves when your hands are cold. Indeed, so downright everyday-practical are some of these encounters that you want to laugh. What's with these angels? They make beds, remind us to buy matches, change flat tires.

I remember once I was in the desert without a hat. The sun beat down unmercifully. I thought, ''I ought to have a hat; I'm going to get sunstroke.'' And four hundred paces ahead, behind a rock, was a battered, torn straw hat. I clapped it on my head. This was before I understood that something—angels, a spiritual cavalry—is watching over us, waiting to be of help. And not to me alone but to all of us and all the time.

I took it as a lucky accident, that hat.

or my birthday one year my husband bought me a gold chain. It was not only beautiful but also unique—each link was a heart connected to another heart. There was only one in the case the day he bought it, and I have never seen another one like it. I always cherished it and wore it often.

One night I took my son to a PTA meeting and decided to wear the necklace. When we got out to the car after the meeting, I realized that the necklace was gone. I went back inside and looked everywhere. I searched and searched. Since we were late getting out of the meeting, the school and parking lot were deserted. I looked everywhere, but no necklace.

The next morning I phoned the school and asked the principal if a gold necklace had been turned in, and of course it had not. He assured me that he would look around the school and let me know if he found it. Several days went by, and no word from him ever came. It was Saturday and rainy. My husband wanted to take me shopping to buy me another necklace, but I wasn't interested; I wanted my necklace back! We decided to go shopping anyway. I'll never forget my thoughts as we drove out of the driveway. I thought if my necklace was outside anywhere, it would be washed away by the rain.

Who provides for the raven his food? When his young ones cry unto God.

—Job 38:41

· · · ·

We went shopping, and when we pulled back into our driveway, it was almost dark. It was still raining lightly. My husband got out of the car first and ran up to the door to open it. When he put his hand on the doorknob, I could see a puzzled look come over his face. I quickly followed and saw what had surprised him: There hanging on the knob was my gold necklace, easily identified by the heart-shaped links.

I called our neighbors (we lived at the end of a dead-end street, so we only had a few) to see if any of them had found the necklace, but since I hadn't told them I had lost it, why should I have expected them to find it, know whose it was, and then bring it back? I also called the principal of the school, but he told me the necklace had never turned up. Several boys in the neighborhood had been outside playing football in the rain, but they hadn't seen anyone come up to our house.

To this day I still have no idea where the necklace was or who was responsible for returning it. The necklace was and still is very special to me. There must have been some significance in my having that necklace, and I will always be grateful for its return.

Donna J. Miller
Chattanooga, Tennessee

OPPOSITE: Pieta. • • • • • • • • • • • • • • • • • •

was about to leave on a trip to Florida. It was a blustery, wet March evening and for some reason I was truly frightened of the plane ride. I was an inexperienced traveler at the time, and I had really worked myself into a nervous state.

Sitting at the dinner table, I thought, "With my luck the plane'll crash." I was trying to make light of my fear, but my throat was tight and I felt like crying. My mother looked at me and said, "You'll have a great time in Florida."

Suddenly, and it seemed to last for a full five minutes, the air was filled with the smell of oranges. It was as though someone had just unpeeled a fat, juicy naval orange directly beneath my nose. The air around the table was rich with the clean, sweet aroma, when just before it smelled of the roast chicken my mother had set down. There were no oranges in the room. Overtaken by this odor, I realized with a sudden calm that, yes, I would get to Florida safely and everything would be fine. I felt completely relieved.

I realize this is almost a comical experience, but it was so real and so unexplainable that I refuse to discredit it.

My final mystical occurrence . . . happened to me about three years ago.

I was attending secretarial school in the evenings in

Rockville, Maryland, and since I lived in D.C., it would often take me an hour to get home. I had no car, so the Metro and a bus ride would not get me to my apartment until long after ten P.M.

One particular night in February the area was experiencing a particularly harsh cold snap with subzero temperatures. Frostbite could take place within a period of twenty minutes.

Leaving school that night, I was dismayed to discover that someone had stolen my good suede and chamois gloves from my schoolbag. I got on the Metro fearing the long wait for an uptown bus. I remember riding the escalator up at Van Ness praying hard to God that a bus would come by soon.

When I came out of the station, the air was so cold, my teeth hurt. I shoved my bare hands into my thinly lined coat pockets and started off toward the bus stop. As I came around a corner, I happened to look directly at one of the garbage cans that are built into the wall. It seemed lit for some reason, and as I walked toward it, I saw a pair of gloves sitting right on top. They were plain brown knit gloves, nothing fancy, but they were clean, and there were two. I plucked them off the top of the can and put them on my already numb hands. I thanked God profusely. The bus didn't arrive until half an hour later.

Again, I realize that these experiences are not as awe-

God created man because He loves the stories.

THE TALMUD

. . . .

inspiring or divine as some (most) that I read in your book, but they have cemented my belief in a Higher Power and the guardians that watch over us.

Elizabeth Ussery
Washington, D.C.

• • • • • • • • • • • • • • • • •

When thou passest through the waters, I will be with thee . . . when thou walkest through the fire, thou shalt not be burned; neither shall the flame kindle upon thee.

—Isaiah 43:2

• • • •

bout a year after my beloved husband died, I sat in my living room feeling lost and lonely—I could not stop weeping. Suddenly the room was filled with the scent of flowers—overpowering. It was in the middle of winter. Just then my phone rang, and it was a friend who wanted to come and visit. I said that I wasn't very good company today, but she came anyway. As she walked in the door, she said, "Where are the flowers?" I said, "Millie, do you smell them too?" With that she asked me, "What was Till's favorite flower?" I said, "Gardenias." She then replied, "He is here with you and telling you not to grieve." With that the scent of flowers disappeared.

Sincerely,

Mrs. Renee E. Mastalli
Bethesda, Maryland

• • • • • • • • • • • • • • • • •

hank you very much for *A Book of Angels*. Your stories gave me encouragement and delight.

Recently I was meditating and experienced a sudden, incredible expansion, or explosion of colors, particles of indigo and gold, into a space so vast I do not have the words to truly describe what this looked like or how I felt . . . except that I was being shown by angels that there is so much wisdom and infinite love within myself! A few weeks after that I started to notice, behind my left shoulder, a brilliant white light, a loving presence. I can "see" it almost any time, and sometimes I have mental dialogues going on, and I feel as though I am being helped and guided through my problems and uncertainties.

The most incredible experience, however, happened just a month or so ago. My four-year-old daughter, Annie, woke up in the middle of the night crying. I went into her room and saw that she had soaked her bed. Stumbling in the half-dark, I grabbed a clean sheet, thinking to myself, "I hope this one fits her bed." I went back to her room and, kneeling by the foot of the bed, I lightly unfurled the sheet, seeing right away that it was a fitted sheet that would fit her mattress. "Thank you, Jesus!" I said to myself. Immediately the sheet was on the bed! All four corners were neatly tucked under! At that same moment

Hold the fleet angel fast
until he blesses thee.
—NATHANIEL COTTON
Tomorrow

• • • •

I sensed, "You're welcome," and I felt a great surge of love. I can't even describe how wonderful it was. Jesus said that to me! Even Annie noticed. She said to me, "Mommy, how did you make the bed like that?" I cried, and I cry now when I remember it. I have tried to tell a few people about this, but I cannot convey to another with words the impact this experience had on me.

I have had other "mystical" experiences, but the one I described above is the one I attribute directly to angels.

Peace to you,

Jennifer Ailstock
Arlington, Virginia

• • • • • • • • • • • • • • • • • • •

Buddhist Angel

y grandmother lived with our family when I was small. Since she was ill, she was always afraid that she'd die and that my brother and I would find her.

I was ten years old and my brother was six on the cold day we entered the house after school and couldn't find our grandmother. We enlisted the help of our neighbor and walked into my grandmother's bedroom. Apparently my grandmother had died in her sleep and lay only a few feet away from us.

However, no one saw her, not even the neighbor lady who was standing with us. My brother, though, said he saw three blue-white angels hovering over the bed. The curtain was up and the room was light. I didn't see them, so I didn't really believe him. To me the bed simply looked as though it was covered with clothes that needed folding.

But later, when I found out that the entire time she lay only a short distance away from us, I knew there'd had to be angels. The angels were there folding the clothes on the bed.

Cynthia Bentley
Milwaukee, Oregon

And since this life our nonage is,
And wee in Wardship to thine
  Angels bee,
Native in heavens faire
  Palaces, . . .
So let me study, that mine actions
  bee
Worthy their sight, though blind
  in how they see.
  —JOHN DONNE
  The Angels, vii

am delighted with *A Book of Angels* and hasten to write to both affirm and thank my angel by telling my most remarkable angel encounter. There are others.

For all of my seventy-six years I have had devotion to my guardian angel. I talk to him as I would my alter ego.

Always busy—teaching full-time at Notre Dame Academy on K Street, District of Columbia, being CCD principal at Saint Bernard's, Riverdale, Maryland, on weekends and raising five children besides—my routine included stopping at Safeway on the way home from school to pick up a few things.

For two days I had forgotten to get book matches. As a smoker, I was forced to light up from the gas stove burner. The third day I gave it a fleeting thought during morning class and said, "Angel, you have *got* to remind me to get those book matches."

That afternoon I shopped at Safeway as usual, picked up my order, and was in line at the cash register, when a voice behind me said *out loud*, "You forgot the book matches."

My legs turned to water as I turned to get a look at my angel. He was an elderly gentleman, with several days' growth of beard, obviously shopping with his wife. She said, "So I did," and rolled her cart to Aisle 4, and I rolled mine right behind her.

It is comforting to know that so many people experience celestial intervention in their lives.

Love in our Angels,

> Regina Ash
> South Bethany, Delaware

We should at all times, and in all places, give thanks to thee, O Lord.

—Book of Common Prayer

• • • • • • • • • • • • • • • • • • •   • • • •

n November 1985 I was traveling with my then ten-year-old daughter to my parents' home, which is a one and a half hours' drive. Dusk was descending as we started up the four-lane mountain highway. Suddenly we heard a loud *pop* and the steering wheel shook as I guided the car off the road onto the shoulder. Getting out of the car, I saw I had a flat tire and was in the middle of nowhere. Down the road about a mile I had seen a small craft store, so I decided we would back up until we came to the store and could hopefully get some help.

I got back in the car and suddenly, it seemed out of nowhere, a car pulled up, and a nice-looking young man got out (my daughter says he was dressed all in white). I showed him my flat tire, and he proceeded to get out the spare, jack, lug wrench, and change the tire. He was very quiet, except for telling me not to stand behind the car in case the jack might fall. Right after he said that the jack did fall, but he quickly finished. I thanked him, offered money, but he refused to take any. I got in my car, he in his, and as I pulled out from the shoulder, my daughter turned around and said, "Mom, he's gone." He had disappeared. Nowhere in sight. He had left as suddenly as he came.

Meg Davis
Greenville, South Carolina

• •

Alaert Duhamel. The Holy Virgin (LEFT) and Saint John (RIGHT) and Angels.

have had, to the best of my recollection, three experiences with angels. I say "angels" because I don't know what else to call them.

The first experience happened in about 1986 in the spring. I live in suburban Maryland and frequently drive to dog shows in Delaware, Pennsylvania, and Virginia, since we breed and show dogs, and I judge some terrier breeds.

On this particular Saturday in May, I drove up the Baltimore–Washington Parkway to connect with I-95 north of Baltimore to attend the dog show given by the Wilmington (Delaware) Kennel Club. On a narrow stretch approaching the Baltimore Harbor Tunnel, I suddenly got a flat tire, and I felt very apprehensive, since there was barely a car's width to stop on the right. I pulled over, not knowing what I would do. My vehicle was a large van and I hadn't used a jack in over twenty years. I secured a white towel in the window and slid out the passenger side, waiting for a policeman to stop and help.

After about a ten-minute wait, a station wagon stopped in front of me, and a rather pleasant-looking man about age twenty-five stepped out and asked if I needed help with my tire. I remember that he didn't smile, and I thought that was odd, since he was kind enough to stop

and help. I thanked him for his thoughtfulness, but told him that he would get awfully dirty, and that if he would just get me to a telephone, I could call AAA, who would come and help. He replied by asking me where my jack and spare tire were, again not smiling. Somehow this frightened me, and I noticed another person seated in the passenger seat of his vehicle. I began to think that they could rob me and leave me on this busy highway. Although the young man had on white shorts and a pale yellow polo shirt, he didn't hesitate to get down on his belly in the dirt to see where he could place the jack. He changed the tire very quickly for his size, and with no difficulty at all. As he stood up to replace the jack, I noticed that his clothes were still sparkling clean. I thanked him again, smiling (although my smile was still not returned), and offered him the twenty-dollar bill in my wallet. He looked into my face and quietly said, "That's not necessary," got into his car, and left. Although this young man was perfectly ordinary in his sports clothes and average blond hair and blue eyes, there was still something disturbingly "different" about him, which left me with such a strong impression. When I returned home that evening, I told my family about my experience, and ended my story with, "I guess that was my guardian angel." I really was helpless in a potentially dangerous situation, and I am convinced that that was why he appeared and helped.

The second "contact" with other-than-human creatures happened one busy morning on my way to the Metro station. I had exited the interstate to a state road to make my connection, when I got myself into the middle of a horrendous gridlock of autos. No one would move because no one *could* move. There were many drivers yelling at each other (one of the most useless activities of all time) accompanied by much horn blowing (equally useless). My own patience ran out as I realized I was going to be late for work if we didn't move, and I stupidly yelled out my van window and blew the horn. Almost immediately a picture entered my mind: it was as though I was standing at the edge of a meadow of green grass and small yellow flowers. The sky was very blue with soft, white, puffy clouds, and there was a sparkling stream running nearby. This was no out-of-body experience, because I was aware that I was still stalled in traffic. I "heard" in my mind a soft voice saying, "He maketh me to lie down in green pastures. He leadeth me beside the still waters. He restoreth my soul." Then, just as quickly, the mental picture faded. I was still in traffic, but it was miraculously beginning to move. I felt a strange peace of mind and calmness as I drove to the station and proceeded to my job. The day turned out to be a hectic one, but for some strange reason I felt this marvelous peace all day. *Nothing* ruffled me, and the peace lasted until I fell asleep that night.

Behold, I send an Angel before thee,
to keep thee in the way.
—EXODUS 23:20

• • • •

The finite mind does not require us to grasp the infinitude of truth, but only to go forward from light to light.

—PETER BAYNE

•   •   •   •

The next day I still had this strong memory of the previous day, and when I contacted my pastor and told him of the *vivid* blues and greens of my mental experience, he quietly said, "C. S. Lewis says that blue and green are the colors of angels. Perhaps the Lord just wanted you to know that, with all the stresses you were going through in your life, the angels were there to uplift you and remind you that you were not alone."

My third memorable encounter—or rather encounters, since it was an ongoing experience—happened repeatedly in a very large subway station, the Metro Center, where four lines converge and I transfer trains. It was not long after my blue-and-green experience that I noticed an older gentleman sitting on one of the benches on the opposite side of the platform. This man bore an amazing resemblance to my father, who had died four months previously. The first time I noticed him, he looked up from his paper and just stared at me. A train came through on his side of the platform, and when it left, he was gone. Over the next year he was not always there, and sometimes when he was, he didn't always get on the train as it stopped. Sometimes he would just watch me until I got on my train. His last appearance was about four months after my divorce, in February 1989, and I have not seen him since, although I always look for him. I actually miss him, probably because he so closely resembled my father, with whom I was very close.

As I said, I have no explanations for any of these occurrences other than to say that they happened when I most needed comfort and assurance.

Barbara J. Anthony
Seabrooke, Maryland

. . . .

 *What are we to make of the silence—or near silence—of these ministering, anonymous spirits? It serves. Indeed in the encounters of near accidents and flat tires (and I received many such accounts) we are aware that what makes the ''angel'' different is his dignity: he does not chat. It is as if human language takes too much energy.*

In other encounters, however, you hear that angels do speak, briefly, and always in the native language of the person hearing it; and sometimes they laugh or smile or play, and sometimes they are heard to sing.

There is another compelling aspect to these stories. The angel comes, often in a human form, does its work . . . and disappears.

n the summer of 1976 I had occasion to drive to Washington, D.C., where my two sisters lived. My stepsister, Betty, and her son, Bradley, who had just graduated from high school, lived in Lawton, Oklahoma. Neither had ever been to Washington, so I invited them to go along, and they accepted. I had a new Lincoln Town Car, which seemed of greater interest to Brad than D.C.

We drove east on Interstate 40 to its intersection with the highway that parallels the Blue Ridge Mountains. On our last day outside of Washington, we had an early dinner in Bristol, right on the Virginia–Tennessee border. The waitress assured us that I-66 was by then finished all the way into Washington. So I continued on to the Front Royal exit and headed east.

The interstate ended a few miles short of Front Royal. We found ourselves on a narrow, back country road that went around barns, made sharp turns that were poorly marked, and was pretty slow going. Eventually, though, it straightened out and I was soon doing about forty miles per hour. It was very dark, the dense evergreen woods contributing to the blackness. Brad was dozing in the backseat. Suddenly Betty yelled, "Look out!" A tall el-

OPPOSITE: Perugino. La Madonna del Sacco.

derly man in a long gray overcoat (it was summer) stepped slowly to the side of the road. He motioned gravely to me to slow down. It was the motion of the hand with the fingers pointing down, not the "Stop!" or "Come!" gesture.

When the car was maybe ten yards away from him, the man just disappeared. He did not step back. He did not move at all. He simply was no longer there.

"Where did he go?" asked Brad, who had awakened at the first shout from his mother.

"He isn't there!" Betty said, as she looked out the back window for him. It was so dark, she probably would not have seen him anyway. Meanwhile I was slowing with the idea of maybe backing up to look for him. But the road made one of those quick turns, and I slammed down hard on the brakes. There, where we would have plowed right into them at forty miles an hour, was a group of twenty or so deer. They were standing in the middle of the road. As my headlights struck them, they slowly ambled off to my left, one or two at a time.

In Washington we tried to tell my sister, Marilyn, about it. She was politely skeptical. So we gave up, and on the way home we took another route, and the subject only came up now and then.

Although I have been a writer almost all of my life, I have never been into fiction. In nonfiction there is usually

. . . it is righteousness—
To believe in God
And the Last Day,
And the Angels,
And the Book,
And the Messengers.
Koran
—s. ii. 177

. . . .

a known ending to the story, and when there is no explanation, that is part of the account. I still have no explanation for the man in Virginia that night.

John Causten Currey
Colorado Springs, Colorado

• • • • • • • • • • • • • • • • •

n the winter of 1972 I was a deacon assigned to a parish in one of our northwest suburbs. Just before midnight one evening I was driving southeast into Chicago during a blizzard. Just as I reached the junction of the Kennedy and the Eden's expressways, where at least eight lanes of traffic converge, my car hit a patch of ice and went into a spin. Applying the brakes made matters worse. As I continued to rotate, I could see the heavy traffic coming toward me. Indeed it seemed that a Volkswagen was about to slam right into me. The car was so close, I could see the other driver clearly, despite all the blowing snow. Bracing myself for the impact, I closed my eyes for a moment and thought, "This is it!" But nothing

My god hath sent his angel, and hath shut the lion's mouths, that they have not hurt me.

—Daniel 6:22

• • • •

Sing, choirs of angels,
sing in exultation,
sing, all ye citizens of heaven
above

. . . .

Annunciation. 14th-Century woodcut.

happened! I opened my eyes. My car had stopped spinning, and directly before me was a big yellow snow-removal vehicle. I could see the hand of its driver, motioning to me that all was okay—that his vehicle would shield me while I turned my car around. He stayed behind me until I was ready to proceed. I remember that, during all this, there was a striking silence and that all the traffic on either side of me continued to dash past. As I began to drive on, I glanced into the rearview mirror and saw his hand waving me a farewell. Then I began to shake violently, having become too internally wound up during this episode. I drove home, convinced that the hand of God had just shielded me from certain death.

There is a sequel to this story. One day, at least seven years later, during my assignment as a priest at Saint Thomas the Apostle Church in Chicago, I asked a class of eighth-graders whether they had ever felt that they had had a personal experience of God. As an example I told them my story. I said that since the winter of '72 a yellow snow-removal vehicle has been for me a symbol of God's loving protection.

The very next afternoon, during a rainstorm, I was driving a friend home from downtown, going south on the Dan Ryan Expressway. My right front tire had a blowout—the only blowout I have ever had. It was no big problem. Since I was in the far right-hand lane, I just pulled off to the side of the road. After the car came to a halt, I glanced in the rearview mirror before opening the door. I was startled to see a big snow-removal vehicle, which had pulled off the road behind me. Its driver climbed out of the cab and came up to me, smiling. He wore a baseball cap. When he asked me if everything was okay, I assured him that things were fine. So he climbed back into his vehicle, gave me a wave, and drove on. Perhaps it's not extraordinary to see a snow-removal vehicle on a balmy day in May.

Thanks for letting me share this.

> Fr. Dennis O'Neill
> Chicago, Illinois

• • • • • • • • • • • • • • • • • • •

Philosophy will clip an angel's wing.

> —JOHN KEATS
> *Endymion*

• • • •

e live in Louisiana. The highways in south Louisiana run on both sides of the bayous.

One afternoon a few years ago my mother and I were going to visit my sister. We weren't really in a big hurry, but we were both annoyed by the woman driving the big car in front of us. She reminded me of my third-grade teacher because she had dark hair pulled up in a bun.

What was annoying was that she kept riding her brakes. There was no reason for her to be braking so much. We were traveling about 45 mph, but she kept slowing down. We thought it was because she didn't know where she was going. I was getting aggravated, because every few minutes she would slow down more, until finally we were going only about 25 mph. Then, she almost came to a stop and turned *right* onto a long shell road.

I watched her for a moment, then looked back at the road. When I looked for her again, she was gone. She had disappeared really quickly for someone who was driving so slowly before.

We drove on, and I felt goose bumps start on the back of my neck. There in the curve an eighteen-wheeler had collided with a small car. The accident had just happened. People were just starting to come out of their houses to help the victims. But the car and truck were in the ditch.

We stared in shock as we passed the accident. Neither of us spoke for a minute. All of a sudden I realized that we were on Highway 308, on the left side of the bayou Lafouche. The highway on the right side of the bayou is Highway 1. The woman couldn't possibly have turned right onto a shell road, because she would have been in the bayou. There *are no* shell roads on the right side, only bayouside homes. Yet we both saw her. She definitely turned right!

I wanted to cry. Was she an angel? She slowed our speed down so much. If we had continued at the same speed, we probably would have been in that accident.

Stephanie Boudreaux
Usouna, Louisiana

. . . .

The word **angel** *means messenger, in both Greek and Arabic. Angels bring warnings, comfort, news. They guard. They help. They heal. They save our lives or carry us away to blessed death. They send us notes or messages that we need; and always they are pointing to something greater than themselves.*

Always they say what angels say, "Don't be afraid. Don't worry. Everything will be all right. We are here." Then they send us the scent of roses or oranges as a sign, or give us a cup of coffee. And they never lay blame on us. They never say, "Boy, are you in a peck of trouble now." They never accuse, "You fool! Look what you've gone and done!" No, but always, "Don't be afraid. We're taking care of things. You're going to like this now."

grew up in a Catholic home, so even as a child I believed I wasn't alone. I remember feeling a presence back then, next to my desk at Saint Gerard Elementary School in Baton Rouge. I don't, however, recall any dramatic instances when the presence became known.

Archangel Raphael. 15th-Century tapestry (detail).

It wasn't until my later years, when I had really screwed my life up, that messages were sent, unspoken prayers were answered, and help from unlikely sources came to my rescue. All this, I think, was the work of angels.

At twenty-four I found myself divorced, without a job, without a home, and without my four-year-old daughter, Sarah, who went to live with my ex-husband.

It was Christmas, the first one away from my daughter, and I was in Houston trying to be sociable at the home of some friends. I had been searching for a job for months without any luck. I was living with my already overburdened parents and I missed Sarah terribly. The guilt was crushing. I doubted I would survive that time.

On Christmas Day I came down with the worst migraine of my life. The pain seared my head for eight hours, and I threw up constantly.

I simply could not endure the pain in my head and my life any longer. As I leaned against the wall of an unfamiliar bathroom, I thought only one word: "Help."

When I looked at myself in a mirror on the opposite wall, I saw a bottle of painkillers that had not been there earlier—pills that were safe for me to take and would ease my incredible pain. I took one and slept peacefully for the next eight hours. In one week I had a job. In several months I moved into my own apartment, and my life began to heal.

But my God shall supply all your need, according to his riches . . .
—Philippians 4:19

• • • •

During those months I frequently heard a woman's voice in my sleep, telling me not to worry, that everything would be all right. I believe it was the Blessed Mother.

Three years later, when I knew I wanted to be married again and start another family, my emotional state again took a dive. I seemed to be attracted to all the wrong men. I no longer trusted my judgment and had given up on dating altogether. Sarah was still with her father and only visited me twice a year. I was very lonely.

One night I dreamed about a man I hadn't seen in years, someone I had gone to high school with. I dreamed we were married, had children, and lived in a two-story house.

The next day his brother called me out of the blue. I asked about Charles and learned that he was away at college but planned to be home soon. Several weeks later Charles called me, and we went to dinner. Three months later we were engaged. A year after that our son was born. And we did purchase a two-story house.

I could go on and on this way. I even consider you an angel of sorts, because your book contains such wonderful messages—information that surely confirms what I suspected all along.

Yvette Z. Patterson
Lake Jackson, Texas

And there appeared a great wonder in heaven; a woman clothed with the sun, and the moon under her feet, and upon her head a crown of twelve stars.
—Revelations 12:1

'd like to tell you a couple of stories.

My husband and I have been married almost ten years. After we'd been married a short time, his problem with alcohol became more pronounced until it cost him several jobs and we were struggling to keep out of debt. I needed spiritual assistance badly. I was trying to juggle bills and money, and it was getting pretty discouraging. One day, from out of nowhere, came a copy of a little pamphlet called "Leaves" that my mother used to subscribe to in our Catholic household. I had no idea who sent it; I didn't subscribe or send for it, even though I was receiving *The Catholic Digest*. But the particular issue I received had a story about Saint Therese, the Little Flower, and how, by saying her novena for five days, you could be granted your request. Then a couple weeks later another "Leaves" came with testimonial accounts from people who regularly prayed to Saint Therese. Then I got no more pamphlets; they stopped as suddenly as they arrived. (I haven't received one since!) In between the issues I got two holy cards with Saint Therese's picture and novena prayer on them. After all these items arrived, I never received another thing concerning Saint Therese.

But this encouraged me to pray the novena, which I still do. It helped me get through some of the darkest

*Silently one by one, in the infinite
meadows of heaven
Blossomed the lovely stars, the
forget-me-nots of angels.*
—HENRY WADSWORTH
LONGFELLOW
Evangeline

· · · ·

hours of my husband's drinking problems. I prayed for him to stop drinking, and he finally did after a year of prayers.

One incident that stands out happened when we were buying our first house, a condominium. We put half of the money down by taking out a loan, but we had to come up with the second half within a few months. I was agonizing about how we'd get the rest of the money, since I couldn't request another loan without being turned down. So I prayed to Saint Therese, asking for her help and then leaving it in her hands for the solution.

It's said that Saint Therese gives you a sign that your request will be answered by leaving a scent of roses or by roses appearing unexpectedly. My sign came when a friend of ours brought me roses from his garden. I felt deeply that this was my sign, but had no idea how this money would come to us. The next morning my husband discovered his van had been stolen. How in the world could this be a good sign? Well, as it turned out, the van had been a total loss. The insurance-company settlement money paid off the remaining portion of the van loan, and the difference left turned out to be the exact amount that we needed to pay toward our mortgage. You can't imagine how amazed and happy I was! I have never doubted the power of prayer, and I know there are those watching over each of us.

Thank you for the opportunity to tell my story and I

hope it can help others who may not be so sure of what's out there. I'm sorry I can't say I have seen any spirits or angels, but I have a very deep faith and I know they are with us.

God bless you!

J. T.
Virginia

. . . .

eside me throughout my life, I have always felt a guiding presence. When I am walking in the wild, as I have done since childhood, this presence guides me and others. I have humorously referred to it as General Direction.

I was raised in the outdoors. I spent ten years in scouting, achieving the rank of Eagle Scout with Bronze Palm. I wandered the woods of the Great Lakes alone all my life, often preferring the company of wild animals to humans. I hunted and fished, paddled and packed, wherever I felt a need or desire to go. So it was not unusual one cold February morning for me to go for a walk outside.

How fading are the joys we dote upon!
Like apparitions seen and gone.
But those that soonest take their flight
Are the most exquisite and strong—
Like angels' visits, short and bright;
Mortality's too weak to bear them long.

—JOHN NORRIS
The Parting

. . . .

The Lord bless you and keep you:
The Lord make his face to shine
   upon you,
and be gracious unto you.

                    Numbers 6:24–25

· · · ·

OPPOSITE: Pollaiuolo.
Tobias and the Angel (detail).

I bundled up in a down parka, boots, hat, and mittens; setting out into the thin, subzero day.

As I left our low-rent student apartment, I mentioned I was off, and no one asked where. I walked down to the shore of a nearby lake, about a mile from home. This lake is nearly twenty-five miles in circumference, nine miles long, and about five miles wide. From where I stood overlooking the bumpy hillocks of ice and snow, I estimated it would take me four hours to reach the middle and return.

The lake had been frozen for two months, and the ice was quite thick. People skied, played, fished, and sailed on it daily. Indeed that day I could see colorful figures off in the distance. I created a line-of-sight target for myself and stomped off into the snow. It was tiring work, and not having been prepared for such a large undertaking, I didn't bring water with me. My thirst increased and I started to eat the snow.

As I reached the turning point, the sky began to cloud over. The cloud cover was unusually low and ominously dark; heavy storm clouds filled the air with large, beautiful, entrancing flakes. The temperature dropped, the wind picked up, and I could no longer see anyone on the ice. Soon I found it difficult to see ahead, and I had to shield my eyes from the stinging snow. I could barely even see my hand in front of my face. I had to lean heavily into the wind. I have no idea how long I walked on

this way. I began to feel cold and drew my hood down tight over my hat. I withdrew my arms from the sleeves up into the chest space. I knew the dangers of hypothermia well.

Stumbling on in the blizzard, I started to fall. At first I figured I needed my arms to balance. Then I realized I could see nothing but white; I had become snow-blind and was confused. When I fell sometimes, I could not stand again. I couldn't differentiate up and down. Better to stay down and crawl, I thought. Occasionally deep, thunderous groans rolled from beneath the surface of the ice. I began calling out for help, only to hear my voice fall dead in the storm before me.

Whether you turn to the right or to the left, your ears will hear a voice behind you, saying: "This is the way; walk in it."

—Isaiah 30:21

• • • •

What if I had been going in circles? I stretched out on the lake, reaching forward, digging in my hands, pulling my knees up and arching my back, inching forward, wormlike. "Please, dear God, help me find my way." Depression began to take hold. I stopped prone in the snow, tears freezing on my cheeks.

Then loud and clear, as if directly before me, came the grand, sonorous foghorn of the rescue station only blocks from my house. "Be careful," said a voice, "the breakwater is open and deep." I moved on again, snaillike, across the bumpy whiteness. After a short while I heard the lapping of gentle waves, closer and closer. "Be careful, stay to the right, climb the concrete wall when you reach it." I heard these things and knew them at the same time;

they were sensible, logical, and, most of all reassuring, like trusted counsel.

Soon the waves were very close, and I removed my glove to feel for wetness near the edge of the ice. My hands were numb, but not without sensation. I found the edge and began moving around to the right, still on my belly, toward the retaining wall. It was beginning to get dark, and, looking up, I faintly saw the light of the rescue station. I felt my way up through the deeply drifting snow to the door. The next thing I felt was being half pulled and half carried inside. A man with dark hair and a beard was there with hot coffee brewing.

After asking me what I was doing, he said he thought he had seen me or someone out on the lake coming in this direction. Thinking the foghorn might help, he set it off. "Good timing," I responded. When I asked him why he was there in the middle of winter, he said he was finishing some research. When I finished my coffee, I decided to go. We said good-bye, and I walked home.

At home I discovered I had been gone for over seven hours and everyone was worried about me. I told them the whole story. My roommate, Dana, said there was no way the rescue station would have been open. The taste of coffee was still in my mouth. "Just a coincidence, I guess!" They thought it was a good story, but given my appearance and physical condition they knew there was some truth in it.

Yea—if ye remain firm,
And act aright, even if
The enemy should rush here
On you in hot haste,
Your Lord would help you
With five thousand angels
Making a terrific onslaught.

Koran
—s. iii. 125

• • • •

The next day, after the storm, in the light of day, I walked back to the rescue building. It was locked up tight, and its concrete-bunker design looked imposing. The door was nearly buried in a drift, which showed no signs of anyone having traveled there. I dug through the drift to the door and read a sign: CLOSED FOR WINTER, with inclusive dates from fall to spring. I called the county sheriff's department and was told no one had access during the winter and no one had been there the day before. I called the university and was surprised to hear the same story.

William N. Lindemann
Tahoma, California

• • • • • • • • • • • • • • • • • •

So many stories. One waitress remembered how when she was a little girl, she got her foot caught in the bedspring and felt invisible hands holding her, freeing her bare foot. . . . Many dying children see angels. "Don't cry," one boy comforted his mother. "Do you see my angel out the window? She's telling me I am going fishing."

One day a contractor came to give me an estimate on work on my house. He saw my newly published book and said, "You should talk to my wife. She's from South America, and when she was a little girl, a little being of light, about six or seven inches high came and played with her and her sister, bouncing on the bed with them. Their mother heard them giggling and she saw light pouring out underneath the bedroom door. She called out, 'What are you doing in there?' But she couldn't open the door until the light faded and the little being had left."

The next writer says better than most how we are only on loan to one another, for a few months, a few years, a lifetime. We cannot try to possess but only enjoy and let our loved ones go.

 have just finished reading your *Book of Angels* and I knew before the end that I was to write to you. I have had a few "experiences" with angels in my past and hesitated to share them out of fear. Your book has opened a dialogue for myself, and countless others I am sure.

There is one incident out of all I have encountered that

Hush! my dear, lie still and
*   slumber,*
Holy angels guard thy bed!
Heavenly blessings without
*   number*
Gently falling on thy head.
                —ISAAC WATTS
Divine Songs: A Cradle Hymn

· · · ·

seemed to be the most important. It involved my youngest daughter, Taryn. We had a home in Hawaii where we were spending the summer of 1986. She was four years old at the time.

It was a very rainy summer, and the kids came down with various colds. Taryn seemed "not well" to me and I took her to the small medical clinic at the end of the island. The doctor there had just finished his residency at Johns Hopkins and was considered quite good. He checked Taryn thoroughly and told me she was fine. A few days later a voice inside told me she was not fine. I took her back to the doctor three times, and each time was told she was all right. Finally a voice said to take her to the hospital on the other side of the island an hour and a half away. I had no way of explaining to my husband or the doctor why I was so insistent.

At the hospital the pediatrician examined her and told me everything looked fine. I demanded that he run blood tests and take X rays. While we were waiting for the results of the blood test, they came and put Taryn on a gurney and rushed her to intensive care. Within minutes they had her on an IV under an oxygen tent. She had a form of pneumonia known as a mycoplasma that responds only to erythromycin. She was down to less than a third of her lung power. They brought me a cot to sleep on in the little private room.

After she fell asleep, I felt I could let down and started

to cry. Then I realized that crying was not how I wanted to spend my energy. I began to pray, listening to the soft hum of the machine pumping oxygen into her tent. As I prayed, an understanding came to me.

This small child that I loved so much was not "mine." She belonged to something much higher and stronger than I, and if she and God had decided it was time for her to leave, there was nothing I could do but be thankful for the time that I had been able to share with our little angel and feel blessed to have had her in our lives. This understanding came with a rush of peace and love that I cannot begin to describe. I felt a light in the room, I opened my eyes and saw a white glow, almost like a cloud around her bed. I felt mesmerized by the light and the feeling of love.

I have always felt that she and God decided that with that understanding she could stay. It was an extremely powerful experience for me and changed the way I looked at my children and life.

(This child was born on All Saints' Day. We named her Taryn because we like the name, and with our last name, the two translate to "Earth Angel.") After this experience I have no doubt that the choice of her name wasn't an accident.

Teddy Seraphine
Evergreen, Colorado

Her angel's face
As the great eye of heaven shined bright
And made a sunshine in the shady place
—EDMUND SPENSER
The Faerie Queen

• • • •

I had been at a speaking engagement in Springfield and was driving east to my home in Columbus, Ohio. Although I had only an hour or so to go, the drive home seemed too long.

The warmth of the spring afternoon sun was just right to drive with the windows down. I longed for scenery this day, so I abstained from using the interstate. It was my habit to drive with the radio off on these trips to enable me to plan my day, contemplate the future and past, and enjoy every inch of the countryside.

The day (what was left of it) seemed like it would be uneventful. The only noticeable sight was an unusually large number of butterflies. They covered the fields for several miles, bouncing gently on the millions of daisies. I surmised this accounted for the black cloud of birds. Little did I know this was a prelude to an encounter I would remember the rest of my life. The birds and butterflies suddenly ascended out of sight. It was then, just ahead, that I saw a hitchhiker. A man. To my surprise he looked much like my father—more than seven years had passed since my father died. I slowed down and pulled over to the side of the road just ahead of him, adjusting the rearview mirror to watch his approach.

ABOVE AND OPPOSITE:
Angels. Romanesque bas relief
(details). (ArchiPhoto)

He drew nearer, and I was shaken. The resemblance was frightening, yet I was drawn to him.

"Dad?" (I don't know why, but I said that aloud.) He was literally a double of my father. He wore khaki pants, black shoes with white socks, and a white T-shirt. He was tall and lean and tan and rugged. His face was my father's face, his hair was thick and black and wavy. I was mesmerized. He walked toward the car in long strides, opened the door, and sat beside me.

He didn't look at me, nor did he speak. The man sat erect and stared ahead, his hands folded in his lap. His manner was nonthreatening. I stared (I'm sure my mouth was open). Imagine seeing your dead father get into the car with you. Was this a ghost or a vivid imagination on a lonesome road?

I put the car in drive and slowly gained speed. Extending my hand, I introduced myself. He returned the handshake. His fingers were long, the palm calloused but warm, very warm. He did not give me his name.

"How far are you going?"

"Not far," he said calmly. It was my father's voice. God, who was this? I was scared. I was intrigued. I was joyous. I was stupid! This was not my father; this was just some old guy hitchhiking. Gain your composure, I kept reciting to myself.

Breathing deeply through my nose and exhaling

*The feather, whence the pen
Was shaped that traced the lives
of these good men,
Dropped from an angel's wing.*
—WILLIAM WORDSWORTH
Walton's Book of Lives

• • • •

through my mouth, I asked, "Where are you going? Are you going to work?"

His answer was direct. "No, I'm visiting with my son. He needs me."

"Where is he?"

"Not far. He is here." He was looking ahead. He turned his head as I did. Our eyes met, and he smiled fully. I nearly cried. His teeth were my father's teeth. His expression was loving. He turned away. My skin crawled. I felt as though I was exposed to a freezing wind and shivered.

"Where do I let you off?"

"This will be fine."

"Here?! It's only been a couple of miles. Does your son live near here?"

"Yes, he is near." His tone seemed patronizing. I pulled over and rolled to a stop. I wanted to plead with him not to go, but deep inside I wondered if what was happening was real.

As he got out, I asked, nearly pleading, "What's your name?" He didn't look at me. He stood close to the car facing me. All I could see was his waist. He did not reply to my question. He stayed there a moment and exhaled deeply. Lowering his head to the window, he revealed a full smile again.

"Thank you." That's all he said. He turned and walked

To me the meanest flower that blows can give
Thoughts that do often lie too deep for tears.
—William Wordsworth
"Intimations of Immortality"

· · · ·

away. He never looked back, although he waved, knowing he was being watched.

I sat in my car for the longest time before pulling away. And driving, I desire to turn around and find him, to follow him. I wanted desperately to see his son.

I pulled over and parked again. Staring ahead momentarily, I finally adjusted the rearview mirror to look at my face.

"You want to see his son? Then look."

I did not know where he was going, nor did I know his name. Or, perhaps I knew all of these things.

I will always remember the visit.

Darrell Smith
Oklahoma City, Oklahoma

. . . .

There is always the question of how to bring the angels to our aid, and story after story affirms what we've been told—that **asking** *is the key.*

Pollaiuolo. Annunciation
(detail).

But just as curious is this: help also comes when we don't even know we are in danger. We are pulled back by invisible hands or we hear a cry of warning in our ears: "Don't move."

Once I asked my teacher how to pray. He answered with a story.

Once there was a dog, which was attacked by a pack of wild dogs. They were snarling, biting, tearing at the poor animal, trying to kill it. It managed to escape and limp home, bleeding, one leg broken. At the door was its master.

What did the dog do? It couldn't speak. It dropped at the man's feet, tail knocking in the dust, and looked at him. And what did the man do but pick up his dog, carry it inside, wash and bandage the wounds, take it to the vet, and give it food, water, and a bed to sleep on. Every day the man changed the dressings, and the dog got better.

The dog did not ask for anything, said my teacher, and that is how we should pray. Presenting ourselves. For if we ask for a shirt, we will get a shirt; and if we ask for a pair of pants we will get a pair of pants. But if we simply present ourselves, our troubled hearts, then we will be given everything we need, and more.

Still, it seems that asking doesn't hurt.

was pleasantly surprised on my birthday when a dear friend of mine presented me with *A Book of Angels*. As I read your book, I found that I have had similar experiences with angels.

I was about twelve years old, living with my parents and two brothers in Pittsburgh, Pennsylvania, when my father lost his job at the J & L Steel Works. He was a devoted employee and felt betrayed by the company, which gave his job to a union employee. He was out of work for what seemed like forever to our family. He tried to find work but ended up with part-time jobs that simply could not put food on the table. Bills piled up, and my mother became very nervous. It was a sad time for a family that was usually in good spirits.

It was about a mile walk to my grade school, past the church where I attended Saturday church school and Sunday services. On the way home from school one day my heart was heavy with the family situation and my father's problems. As I came upon the church, I decided to go in and pray for help for my father. I reached the front door, found it unlocked, and entered the quiet, empty nave. While walking up the center aisle, a very strange feeling came over me, somewhat like a drunken state when you forget all your problems. I prayed, and I knew that my prayer would be answered. I walked home without a care in the world, and when my mother told me that my father had found work that very day, I decided to keep my experience secret. This is the first time that I have felt moved to tell this story. As a child I felt if I told the story, my father would lose the job that the angels had given him. By the way, weeks later our pastor stopped me and said that he had seen me praying in the church and asked if he could help. I said that my prayers had already been answered. He then asked me how I had gotten into the church and explained that all the doors had been locked.

Forty years have gone by. I became an art teacher, I married, and have two wonderful sons.

When I had my second angelic experience, it was eleven P.M., and I was alone in the kitchen. My son, Dean, had called me during the day to ask me to send some résumés to prospective employers. He had been driving eighteen-wheelers for a national company and had started to hate his job. He missed home and his girlfriend and wanted to find a local place to work—a difficult task because unemployment is high in our area. After posting two letters he wanted to send, I could not find the third address. I opened the yellow pages for help and found that it had opened to a page of building suppliers. Suddenly that feel-

Guardian Angel.

Then our mouth was filled with laughter,
and our tongue with singing.
                    Psalms 126:2

• • • •

ing of forty years earlier warmed up inside me. The name of one local supplier stood out. I felt so confident that this company would hire my son, that I wrote a letter in his name asking for a job. A few weeks later Dean quit his job. I told him what I had done, and he replied that he didn't think that the company had any job openings. I still was confident about the feeling I had and prayed in church on Sunday that a job would open up for him. On Monday morning the phone rang and Dean was asked to come in for an interview and the next day had the job. The day the letter arrived, an employee had quit his job, and they needed help immediately.

Perhaps the angels have an unemployment office. In any case I can't explain these happenings, but I seem to understand that I need not ever explain them, for they bring peace and are done through love. In fact they do not seem odd to me. When I remember the happenings, they seem natural and warm. This is why I have written this letter, for when I read your book, these feelings were there, and when I decided to write this letter, these feelings returned.

Sincerely,

Dean Marshall
Harmony, Pennsylvania

• • • • • • • • • • • • • • • • • • •

n September 20, 1990, my three-year-old little girl went outdoors to play. As I watched through the sliding-glass patio doors, she opened the back door, turned to close it, and then squatted down almost immediately. I turned away, and a few moments later heard a crash. A huge limb had fallen from our largest elm tree, right near my little girl.

Later, I asked my daughter why she hadn't been playing in the yard, driving her little, red, battery-powered jeep. She said without any hesitation, "Mommy, a good god told me to sit down and not go under the tree, and I did just what she told me to do." This "good god" was a beautiful girl with long golden hair that flowed past her shoulders. She came from the sky and had wings. She had a light so bright about her, said my daughter, that it hurt her eyes, but, when she touched the light, she was surprised how cool it was. It did not burn. The angel had specific jewelry on, especially a necklace that was "so shiny." She wore, said my daughter, "all colors."

Certain changes have occurred in my daughter's behavior since the incident, most noticably a serene calmness. She prays for her angel and also insists on saying a grace at every meal, a tradition that had not been in our family before. She has drawn numerous pictures of "Rebecca

Rose" almost every day since the incident, and wants stories of the Bible read to her at night.

Now, several more months have passed. She says that she cannot see "Rebecca Rose" anymore—is not allowed to—and she longs to have her back; but she says that she has been told she will see her again in ten years.

Name withheld by request
Las Vegas, Nevada

. . . .

am now seventy-six years old, and I can't resist writing you about an experience I once had.

One day, years ago, when I was working at the Smithsonian, I had gone uptown during lunch hour. When I returned, I walked down Tenth Street to E and paused at the curb, waiting for the light to change. Suddenly someone put a firm hand on my right shoulder and pulled me back so hard and fast that I nearly fell. At the same instant a city bus on Tenth Street turned right on E and crossed over the curb and directly over the spot where I had been standing. I turned to thank my rescuer, and *no*

OPPOSITE:
Archangel Michael.

one was there. There was no one anywhere *near* me, as I had been the only person waiting to cross there. I looked around, stunned, for several minutes, then slowly went on to work, but I knew that no living person had helped me. I think I was really in a state of shock the rest of the day.

Bethune M. Gibson
Sedona, Arizona

. . . .

 *Here is the story of a boy who saw his sister's guardian-angel playmate, though we don't know if she, Linda, was aware of the presence or not!*

y first experience with an angel happened when I was twelve years old, back in 1973. My sister, Linda, was returning from school one afternoon, and I was looking through the peephole of our apartment to see her when she got off the elevator. When Linda stepped off the elevator, I saw a blond teenage girl dressed in the same school uniform that Linda wore. The blond girl walked very close behind Linda. I didn't think much of it, because Linda attended an all-girl's high school and she always came home with one friend or another. Anyhow I rushed to open the door, but I saw only Linda standing there. I asked her about her blond friend, and she informed me that she was alone. Well! That's when I came to the conclusion that I had just seen an angel.

Years before I saw the angel, my two other sisters, Carmen and Cookie, saw a blond little girl sleeping next to Linda one night. They dared not disturb her. They knew she was an angel, but something told them not to disturb the sleeping child. They went back to sleep, and in the morning the angel was gone!

Joey Román
Tarzana, California

*And out of darkness came the hands
That reach through nature, molding men.*
—ALFRED, LORD TENNYSON
In Memoriam

he year was 1938, and it was a cold, wet, dreary February afternoon. I was a sixteen-year-old boy who had been on the road for over four months. Life on the road in those Depression years was hard, and I was trying to get home. The place was the railway yards in Hayti, Missouri. I was standing under the shed of a warehouse loading dock waiting for the freight train that was in the yards taking on water and coal to start moving out. You don't climb into a boxcar while the train is in the yards because the railroad bulls will hit you over the head with a club and kick you off.

The train started moving out, pulled by two large locomotives, which meant that it would gain speed quickly and that it was a long train.

I stood waiting until I saw a boxcar with a door open, then I started running to jump in. The boxcar was rather high off the ground because of the terrain. When I jumped, I only got halfway in, the lower half of my legs dangling out of the door and the upper half of my body lying flat on the floor of the boxcar. I couldn't pull myself in because I had nothing to hold onto. The train was gaining speed very fast as I lay there trying to pull myself in, my arms outstretched on the floor. I knew if I fell it

There was a time when meadow,
grove, and stream,
The earth, and every common
sight,
To me did seem
Apparelled in celestial light,
The glory and the freshness of a
dream.

    .   .   .

Our birth is but a sleep and a
forgetting:
The Soul that rises with us, our
life's star,
Hath had elsewhere its setting,
And cometh from afar:
Not in entire forgetfulness,
And not in utter nakedness,
But trailing clouds of glory do we
come
From God, who is our home:
    —WILLIAM WORDSWORTH
    "Intimations of Immortality"

.   .   .   .

would be certain death under the wheels of that freight train. I will never forget that moment. I thought my time had come.

As I was struggling on the floor, I can recall saying, "O God, please don't let me die here." I raised my head enough to see a very large black man, in his thirties, standing there looking at me. He didn't say anything to me and I didn't say anything to him. He reached down, got hold of me by the arms, and pulled me into the boxcar. I lay on the floor facedown for about half a minute to catch my breath and regain my strength. When I got up to thank the man, he was nowhere to be seen. The boxcar was completely empty; the other door was closed, and the train was moving too fast for anyone to jump out and live. There was no one in that boxcar but me. The black man had vanished.

If a person has his own guardian angel, then my angel is a big, strong, black man in his thirties who saved me from a sure death at the wheels of a freight train and didn't wait around to be thanked.

    Charles A. Galloway, Jr.
    Jackson, Mississippi

. . . .

grew up hearing the following story from my mother. In fact my mother told the story so often and so vividly that I was able to picture the two visits from the mysterious stranger as clearly as though I had been present.

On a cold, crystal-clear Christmas morning in 1911 (my brother's second birthday), my mother answered a knock at the front door to find, standing on the top step of our front porch, a handsome, well-dressed man and a pretty little girl. Standing at the child's side was a large white dog.

The stranger greeted mother by wishing her a Merry Christmas and inquiring about my brother's health. Mother told him that my brother had been in very good health but had awakened that morning with a slight fever.

"I know," the man answered, "but he will recover shortly."

At this point in the story we children always asked, "Why didn't you ask him his name?" Mother always answered patiently, "I did ask him his name and I pleaded with him to come in out of the cold, but he just smiled and shook his head no."

Although the man had cautioned Mother to close the

William Blake. Angel.

How like an angel came I down.
—THOMAS TRAHERNE
Wonder

. . . .

door against the cold, she waited to see in which direction the trio would walk, hoping for a clue to the identity of her visitors. Just as the three reached the last step, my father called from the kitchen. My mother turned to answer him, and when she looked toward the street again, it was empty, with no sign of the man, the little girl, and the dog.

Of course the visit from the mysterious stranger was the subject of conversation among our family and friends for months, but no one ever came up with a clue to his identity.

The incident was almost forgotten when, in April 1914, the stranger made his second visit. Just as had happened almost three years before, he was standing on the top step of the porch when mother answered the door. Just as before he declined Mother's invitation to come into the house, nor would he tell his name.

"I'm sorry about your husband losing his job," the man said, "but he will be working again soon."

This time the man turned toward the deep woods at the back of the house. Mother ran down the steps after him, but by the time she got to the back of the house, the area was as quiet and serene as always, with no sign of anyone, just the tall trees swaying in the April breeze.

He must have the wrong house, Mother thought, when she went back into the kitchen. She thanked God that it was not her husband who was out of work. When my

Wilt thou love God, as he thee!
  Then digest,
My Soule, this wholesome
  meditation,
How God, the Spirit, by Angels
  waited on
In heaven, doth make his Temple
  in thy brest.
                    —JOHN DONNE
                    Divine Poems XV

• • • •

father came home that night, he told Mother that he had been laid off! When Mother removed her apron that night and went through the pockets getting ready to put it in the wash, there was a twenty-dollar bill in the right-hand pocket.

What was it all about? Why did the man come on two separate occasions almost three years apart? Who was he? How did he know so much about our family?

I wish I could say that Mother's life changed for the better after the stranger's visits—it did not. I guess the one good thing about the two visits was that the man became a symbol of hope. Whenever money was short in our family and things were desperate, we told each other, "Maybe the man will come." He usually did—in one form or another.

Marie Grant
Jamesburg, New Jersey

• • • • • • • • • • • • • • • • • • • •

Earlier Joey Román saw his sister's guard-ian angel, but here two adults saw an angel in the hospital and received its compassionate help in accepting death.

Perhaps what we are to understand is this: there is no death and we do not die. Many, many are the people who wrote of seeing their loved ones after they died, or feeling their presence, or being visited by them from the Other Side.

Farther on we read of the nine-year-old boy who saw an angel (but was it one?) beside his hospital bed weeping "as if his heart were breaking."

What are we to make of this?

 was in the bookstore the other day when your book, *A Book of Angels*, jumped off the shelf at me, so of course I bought it. With all that's happened to me in this life I no longer need a building to fall on me to get the picture. One blessing I feel that I am getting the hang of is listening to that divine presence that's with us all. What a relief.

It seems now, at thirty-seven, as I look back on my life, so many wonderful spiritual beings and lessons have come my way, at times cloaked in tragedy. And though I carry a few emotional battle scars, as a whole I think I'm doing rather well. At least I am on the path and my eyes and heart are open.

I have had more than my share of ghosts, invisible caresses, voices of encouragement and love, which at some time I might be able to pass on to you, but today I have to tell you about one angel in particular I met.

In 1981 my twenty-eight-year-old husband was diagnosed as having acute lymphatic leukemia. Chris (my husband) and I were living in Nashville, Tennessee, and were told by doctors that his only chance of survival was through a bone-marrow transplant. They felt we needed to go to Houston's cancer hospital, M. D. Anderson, for treatment.

Living in a cancer hospital is a story in itself, which I won't go into here. Just know that we spent a year living there, and, yes, it was a nightmare. Death and sorrow at every turn.

Anyway, on with why I'm writing. On January 4, 1982, at three A.M. I was awakened by a nurse telling me that Chris was gone! Yes, gone. I need to say two things here. First, the nurses' station is an island on a circular floor surrounded by rooms. To get to the main hall and elevators without being seen would not be easy, especially if you were attached to two I.V. poles on each arm. In addition Chris had been too weak from his last dose of chemo to walk without help.

Also, for the first time in a year, for some unknown

reason, I slept as if I was in a coma. Prior to that night I was at his side if I heard a pin drop on the floor! I was in tune to this man's needs, awake or asleep. My cot, when folded out for the night, was maybe eight inches away from his bed.

The nurses were a bit shaken. I jumped up and took off down the hall. We were on the eleventh floor in the intensive care unit for different kinds of blood-related cancers, mostly leukemia. As I made my way toward the elevators (which by the way were patrolled by security after nine P.M.; you had to have an I.D. card to even enter the hospital), my eye caught movement through the glass panel in the eleventh-floor chapel. I went to the door and peeked in, I couldn't believe it—there was Chris with his back toward me sitting with a man.

First I was mad, because I had been frightened, then I was scared because who was this man? He was not any-one I had seen before. Where did he come from at three in the morning? When I entered the very small room, his eyes went to the floor, and I felt that he did not want me to see his face. I was suspicious. I was talking to Chris, but I was trying to get a look at this man. "Chris," I said, "where have you been?"

This man had on a red-checked flannel work shirt, blue jeans, and brand-new lace-up work boots. His hair was cut in a burr cut and was white; his skin was white; he had the appearance of being transparent! Only once did

OPPOSITE:
Hans Memling. Angels.

our eyes meet, and his were ice blue. I could not keep my eyes off this guy. I studied and studied him, for lots of reasons, first because he was here with Chris, and Chris was smiling and laughing and seemed so strong, and also because I wanted to make sure he was not dangerous. Then Chris spoke, "Melissa, it's okay, I'll be back in the room in a little while."

"What's going on?" I asked.

"Melissa, please, I'll be back in the room soon."

I looked at his face and could tell he was all right. I could also tell he really wanted me to leave.

I went back to the nurses and told them I had found Chris in the chapel. They were very relieved. I waited about thirty minutes. When Chris returned, he was happy and full of energy. Chris let me fire questions away at him until, still grinning, he said flatly, "Melissa, he was an angel." He was so happy. I looked him straight in the eye and said, "I believe you," and I did.

It seemed Chris had been summoned, I had been put in a deep sleep, and the nurses for some reason just didn't see him when he passed by.

Chris told me that he just jerked awake and had this overpowering urge to go to the chapel. He was on his knees praying in the chapel when this voice asked him if he was Chris Deal, and he said yes. He never heard this man enter the room, but when he turned around, the man was there. They sat across from each other, their knees almost touching. The man asked him if he needed forgiveness for anything. Chris told him of his hatred for his stepfather, and that he wanted to be able to forgive him. The young man told Chris he had been forgiven. He told the man he was worried about me, and the man said not to, that I was going to be fine. Then Chris said the man asked him if he would like to say the rosary with him, (he somehow knew that Chris was Catholic). They both knelt at the altar and said the rosary, and when they were through, the man told Chris not to worry, that all his prayers had been answered.

At that I took off down the hall to the chapel, but the man was gone. I went down in the elevator, where I met a security guard. I gave him the young man's description, but he said the man had not come by him. I guess he could have gotten off at another floor, but Chris laughed at me when I mentioned that.

The next day Chris was happier and more energetic than I had seen him in months. Somehow the weight of carrying around a terminal illness had left him.

On January 6 I awoke to find Chris lying on his side in his bed just staring at my face.

"What?" I asked.

"I dreamed of Bill B. last night." Bill was Chris's best friend, who had died in a car wreck a year earlier. I had

It seems to the soul that the entire universe is a sea of love in which it is engulfed, for, conscious of the living point or center of love within itself, it is unable to catch sight of the boundaries of this love.

—ST. JOHN OF THE CROSS
The Living Flame of Love

• • • •

Gustave Doré. Illustration
from *The Divine Comedy*

once told Chris that if he ever dreamed of Bill, I wanted
to know. For some reason I knew that Bill would come
for Chris if he were going to die. I knew I didn't have to
worry, unless Chris dreamed about Bill.

"What about the angel?" I asked.

"You told me to tell you if I ever dreamed about Bill,"
he said. I never mentioned why I wanted him to tell me
about Bill, but I could tell by the way he studied my face
that he knew why.

That afternoon Chris had a pulmonary hemorrhage and
died calling my name.

I have now, after six years, remarried and moved to
Atlanta. I am very happy. Needless to say, my memories
are always with me.

Kindest regards,

Melissa Deal Forth
Atlanta, Georgia

. . . .

ixteen years ago I was driving home alone
from my uncle's funeral. This uncle had helped raise me
when I was a little girl because for a time my mother

could not. He had always been an honest, hardworking, responsible man and was extremely independent. Under his straight-backed Scandinavian seriousness was a heart of gold. He had worked hard all of his life until one day he had a stroke.

For a time my aunt tried to care for him at home, but her health finally gave out, and he was put into a convalescent home. This fiercely independent man now had to depend on strangers for everything. Each day of the next ten years must have been like living in hell for him.

On the way home from the funeral I somehow took a wrong turn. I ended up on a beautiful country road winding through the vineyards that he loved so much. As I drove along, I started to talk to him. I visualized him as a butterfly flying free at last and I told him that I loved him.

Almost at the moment I thought of him as a butterfly, dozens of butterflies flew in front of the car. They stayed with the car for a short distance, and then they were gone.

I had the feeling that my uncle had found a way to reach me and let me know that he was happy at last.

Elise Smith
Freestone, California

• •

Methinks we have hugely mistaken this matter of Life and Death. Methinks that what they call my shadow here on earth is my true substance. Methinks that in looking at things spiritual, we are too much like oysters observing the sun through the water, and thinking that thick water the thinnest of air. Methinks my body is but the lees of my better being. In fact take my body who will, take it I say, it is not me.

—HERMAN MELVILLE
Moby Dick

• • • •

recently read *A Book of Angels* and enjoyed it very much. I thought I would write and tell you about something that happened to me when I was younger.

One evening in 1974, when I was nine years old, my mother and I were preparing to go to a movie. We took the Volkswagen Beetle and were heading for town, when we were run into head-on by a sixteen-year-old boy. Our car was destroyed; I was pitched through the windshield, broke both my arms, cut up my face, and received a concussion. My mother died.

I do not remember any of this. The last thing I remember before the accident was looking at the newspaper and telling my mother that the movie started at seven-thirty.

My next memory is of waking up in the recovery room of the hospital. I felt groggy and dull, I guess because I was coming out from under general anesthesia. To the left of my bed, near my head, I saw someone sitting in a chair—a young man maybe eighteen years old with shining blond hair. He was dressed all in white and was holding his head in his hands and weeping as if his heart were breaking. At the foot of my bed sat my father and my older brother. I remember seeing the person near my head first, then I looked at my dad. "Where's Mom?" I asked.

"She's in heaven," my dad said.

The full impact of this statement didn't hit me until sometime later in the day, after my dad and brother had left. I had to go to the bathroom, and I guess it hadn't quite hit me that I was in the hospital and should ring for a nurse, so I got up. I remember being very surprised that I could hardly stand, and I was truly shocked, to the point of nearly fainting, when I saw my face in the mirror. The area near the left corner of my mouth looked like raw hamburger, and my left eye was almost completely swollen shut. (I found out later that, had the glass of the windshield struck a quarter inch closer to my nose, I would have lost my eye.)

I recall suddenly becoming convinced that it was all a bad dream, so I staggered out into the hall to see if I could get myself to wake up. There followed the predictable hysteria on my part, and I was herded back to my bed by a kindhearted nurse.

It didn't occur to me until many years later that I had no idea who had been weeping at the side of my bed. At first I thought, "The person was wearing white, so it had to have been a nurse." However, I was fairly certain that it was a man, and male nurses aren't all that common; and even if it was a nurse, surely nurses are somewhat inured to tragedies and wouldn't weep at the bedside of a total stranger.

No members of my immediate family or friends of the family were blond. And I'd never seen such a beautiful, glossy blond color either, before or since. Even though I was very groggy, I could see how brightly his hair shone.

And why was he wearing white if he wasn't a nurse? Reflecting on it later, I realized that I'd gotten the impression, strangely enough, that he was wearing a tuxedo. I do not, however, recall whether he had wings.

Strangely, at the time it happened, I didn't wonder about any of this. I accepted him and never thought to ask anyone, "Who was that?" I suppose I should ask my father or my brother, but I don't know if they would remember, and truthfully I'm scared to ask. I don't know if they saw him, but I saw him just as clearly as I saw them.

Another odd thing is that I've been told repeatedly that I nearly died after the accident. I didn't think the injuries I received were all that serious; of course the concussion could have turned into something worse, and I might have lost the left eye, but I was fortunate on both counts. I do know that Mom and I went to see the movie on July 2, and I woke up on July 4. I've never been able to get a straight answer on why or how I nearly died or why I lost a day.

I've more or less come to the conclusion that that must have been an angel sitting beside my bed. Maybe he gave me something, or took something from me, so that I could live. Maybe, in the final scheme of things, my

There shall no evil befall thee, neither shall any plague come nigh thy dwelling.

—Psalm 91: 10

. . . .

mother had to die so that other events could take place. I suppose I'll never really know for sure.

I wish this story had a more definite ending or that the angel had appeared to me in a more dramatic or positive fashion. I will always have scars on my face and a void in my heart, but at least someone cared enough to sit beside me for a few minutes.

Sincerely yours,

Corky Visminas
Columbus, Ohio

. . . .

 *Not long ago there was a time when I was in distress, not knowing how to find my way. I prayed to know what to do. Later that day, attending a meeting (and still in pain), I heard very faintly through the wall behind me the most beautiful clear voice singing on the radio, or so I thought. The voice was so sweet, I held my breath to listen. It sang three pure descending notes, then stopped, repeated the three notes again, and stopped again. No one*

else in the meeting seemed to hear, but my heart was pierced by those three notes.

The singing stopped. Apparently it was not a radio.

All day those three clear notes hung in my ear. I kept trying to recall the music they suggested, until suddenly that evening I remembered they were from a chant sung at the National Cathedral: "Ah . . . ah . . . ah . . . Adoramus te, Domine." (We adore you, Lord; let us adore you, Lord.) My heart lifted.

It was the answer to my prayer. In trust my distress would ease. Now I cannot forget that voice.

Several people wrote of hearing a voice speak to them or direct them to do something. In some cases it gives information of what will come to pass, as if our destiny is predetermined, as if there is a fate! In other cases it simply sings. But beautifully! In the next story a very sick child hears voices singing in choirs, and at the end, years later, comes a miracle.

 recently bought your book, and I am overwhelmingly compelled to write you!

In 1960 I was born with what is still considered a fatal heart defect. My parents were not given much hope. I had open-heart surgery at the age of six months but the doctors said I would not live much longer.

When I was seven years old, I woke up early one morning and was looking out of the window in our living room. It was early November. I remember it started like someone ringing a little bell far away, then, ever so softly, I heard a choir of the most beautiful voices I have—or *ever again will*—hear singing. At first I couldn't make it out, but then I could recognize "Hark the Herald Angels Sing," "Joy to the World," and more muted singing before it faded. At this time the only Christmas songs I was *very familiar* with were "Silent Night," "Jingle Bells," "Santa Claus Is Coming to Town," and "Frosty the Snowman"! I knew these other songs existed but had not known them word for word.

A few weeks later I started to have a cough and run a low-grade fever—99 to 100 degrees—enough for a mom to keep a seven-year-old with a heart defect at home. I was sitting on the couch looking out into our backyard when I heard that little bell again, and then the sweet singing of those same songs.

I called my mom and asked if she could hear those angels singing and I couldn't understand why she said she couldn't—it was so soft and so clear! It sounded like someone had left the radio on and the music was drifting across the living room. (Mom now admits I scared her to death.)

The angel's singing came and went for days—always

It came upon a midnight clear,
That glorious song of old
From angels bending near the
*   earth*
To touch their harps of gold.

• • • •

*Still through the cloven skies they
 come,
with peaceful wings unfurled,
And still their heav'nly music
 floats
o'er all the weary world:
Above its sad and lowly plains
they bend on hov'ring wing,
and ever o're its Babel wounds
 The blessed angels sing.*

· · · ·

OPPOSITE: Master of Moulins.
Virgin and Child.

when it was quiet and I was alone. I had been home for several weeks with this fever—and also an abscessed tooth. One afternoon I was sitting in my room playing with my dolls when the angelic singing started up. By now I had grown used to it. This time the singing was a little louder, but there was one voice that was particularly off-key. It annoyed me, and as if it knew, the off-key voice kept singing louder and louder until it was the only one I could hear. This terrified me, and I went out of the room screaming for my mother. I tearfully tried to explain to my mother what had happened. Mom kept asking if this "voice" called my name or told me to do anything. By this point she probably thought I was losing my young mind.

I never again heard the singing. Shortly after all of this I was put into the hospital with bacterial endocarditis—an infection of the lining of the heart stemming from the abscessed tooth. The doctors told my parents that the infection was so severe, I would probably die and that they would keep me comfortable so that my death would be painless.

I was released from the hospital on December 24, 1967, free of the infection.

I had open-heart surgery for the second time at the age of twelve. Again the doctors told my parents that due to the nature of my defect I would probably not live through my teens. I had surgery again at the Mayo Clinic at the

age of twenty-six and a half. The doctors were amazed with me—I kept hearing the phrase "lucky to have made it this long."

I am now a happily married thirty-year-old living in the Maryland suburbs of D.C. My friend who knows about "my angels" said that she thinks when a child is in danger, angels are sent to protect him or her. Since children are so innocent, they can sometimes hear these angels, who are constantly singing in praise of God.

I was facing heart surgery again this winter. I was not at all scared, just concerned for my *very worried* husband. But let me finish my story.

I was in Georgetown Hospital almost the entire month of November.

I was hospitalized because a routine exam showed a blockage in my aorta (called a stenosis). They did several echocardiograms—sonograms of the heart. Each "echo" showed the stenosis. The doctors came to the conclusion that surgery would definitely have to be done to remove the stenosis. They would have to do one more test, a catherization, and inject dye into the main artery and watch it circulate through the heart, to determine the actual size of the stenosis and how urgently surgery was needed.

I was awake through the procedure, and my cardiologist talked to me all through it. When the dye circulated to the part of the heart where the stenosis was, he stopped dead, looked at me, and said, "I can't believe this. There's nothing there!"

He looked again and called in other doctors to look. Of course the medical world, being what it is, *cannot* understand what happened and *will not* admit to divine intervention.

My husband, family, and I are overjoyed and praise God every day. My dad said he was not at all surprised because the day before my last procedure he lit a candle for me and told the Blessed Virgin that I had been through enough. The *day* of the procedure my mother, knowing my fondness for angels, gave me a tiny gold angel pin to wear on my gown while the procedure was being done.

The choirs of angels who sang to me as a child have touched my life deeply and affected me (obviously) ever since. I have heard many choirs, and none of them could compare to those beautiful voices I heard in '67.

Name withheld by request

· · · · · · · · · · · · · · · · · · · ·

Angel. Spanish manuscript illumination.

hen I was living and working in Manhattan in 1960, changing from one job to another in the high-powered world of advertising and photography, I went to the New Jersey shore to refresh myself. I met a man there, a young doctor, who was between residencies. He had six weeks to recoup before leaving for the Mayo Clinic and was living in a shore house. He asked to take me out in the city the following Tuesday night. I realized I had forgotten his last name. He wrote it in the sand in two layers: EDEL MANN. I heard a strong male voice to my right announce, "You'd better remember that. It will be yours." I looked all around. There was no one else within speaking range. And the voice was right, this man proposed within the month.

Sincerely yours,

Carolyn Foote Edelmann
Princeton, New Jersey

· · · · · · · · · · · · · · · · · · · ·

have read only about a third of your *A Book of Angels* and had to write.

Since I learned about angels fifteen years ago, I have been aware of them as constant companions, guiding and inspiring my thoughts, giving warnings, reproof, comfort, solace, advice. All in nonintrusive, subtle ways.

I don't have great, amazing stories of them appearing or moving me from one place to another, but instead, the sense of their constant presence, quietly prompting little things, like what to pack for the day's outing, what to say to the kids about a problem, which way to go in a million little decisions. Very often I feel a pressure on my right ear if I am getting a "green light" to say or do something—and a pressure on my left ear if I am being warned *not* to do something.

Just using that term *green light* reminded me of an incident before I was married. My (now) husband then had no real attraction to me, but I had had numerous dreams and strange coincidences that told me clearly that we would one day be married. This went on for some time, and though we were both friends and saw each other a lot, I never mentioned any of those things to him. How embarrassing, I thought!

There's not the smallest orb which thou behold'st
But in this motion like an angel sings,
Still quiring to the young-eyed cherubins
Such Harmony is in immortal souls;
But, whilst this muddy vesture of decay
Doth grossly close it in, we cannot hear it.
—WILLIAM SHAKESPEARE
The Merchant of Venice

• • • •

Then, the night before he was coming to my house for a casual dinner, I had a dream that he came up to me and gave me a kiss on the right side of my nose. I awakened, and the angel said clearly to me to look up *nose* in Ann Ree Colton's book *Watch Your Dreams*. I did and found among her writing on this symbol:

When one receives the constellation etheric touch to the right nostril, he is being told by his Guardian Angel to go ahead; this is a "green light" signal from the higher worlds.

Since he touched me on the right side of the nose, I knew the angels were telling me to go ahead and tell my husband-to-be about my inner experiences.

I did. And in a matter of months we were married.

We've been married twelve years and love each other more all the time and have two beautiful daughters, who share our spiritual life with us.

This is only one of the thousands of ways that angels have made their help and presence known to me. One thing—the more I say thank you to them, express my gratitude, the more I become aware of them. So I try always to be mindful of expressing gratitude.

Angels also work through "coinciding." These "coincidences" occur in countless ways. You hear a word on the radio at the same time you're looking at it on a piece of paper; you're talking or thinking about a person, and a license plate pulls in front of you with the person's name or initials on it; last night you had a dream about Indians, and first thing in the morning you see a huge truck with an Indian painted on it; something just happened to you that was very out of the ordinary, and just afterward you see a movie or read in a book of that same unusual thing happening to someone else. It goes on and on.

The angels are masters of time and work with you through these little time miracles.

From a grateful and respectful reader.

Tayria Ward
La Crescenta, California

• • • • • • • • • • • • • • • • • • • •

Remember ye implored
The assistance of your Lord,
And He answered you:
"I will assist you
With a thousand of the angels,
Ranks on ranks."

Koran
—s. viii. 9

• • • •

William Blake. From
"Illustrations for the
Book of Job."

Why do angels like disguise? They come as visions, voices, dreams, coincidences, and intuition, the whisper of knowledge at your ear. They come as animals or other people, or as a wash of peace in an ailing heart. Sometimes a stranger may come up and give you just the information or assistance you need. Sometimes you yourself are used as an angel, for a moment, either knowingly or not, speaking words you did not know you knew.

But sometimes these beings come as angels, in the very form that artists show—as beings of light, both with and without wings. Those who have seen them do not always agree on how they look. They are male or they are female; they are large or small; adults or children.

They stand, doing nothing, only looking in a puzzling way at the person who observes them; or else they weep (imagine!), or else they demonstrate a truth or bring a word of hope. And it is not to saints they come, but to ordinary people.

In the next letters a six-year-old sees six angels and, terror-struck, wants to stay alive! It is the only letter I received in which an angel does not bring peace and comfort or play or fun. In other accounts a grown woman sees an angel watching her—with no message at all—and still another is given a mystical revelation of the profoundest kind.

have had an experience that throughout the years has remained "my mysterious precious moment." I have guarded this, discussed it once with a clergyman, and passed it on to a sister, one of my children, and a friend or two. The reaction was silence, maybe a few questions; and whatever else their thoughts were, I know not.

One thing I do know is that it never, ever mattered to me whether I repeated this or not, for I never felt the need to make anyone understand, believe, or even discuss it. I knew it happened, and when it happens to you, you just "know" it to be true. This is all that matters, and you can hold this mystery in your heart and soul forever and ever.

I hope I can pass this on with the love and esteem that I hold for this experience. I was a young married person in my early twenties, in my first little frame home. I can tell you where every piece of furniture in my bedroom was placed, how I was sleeping, and I still see myself and my *dear angel* when she came. It was during the night. My bed was facing west, and I was on the right-hand side. The room did not open up, the sky did not part, the room did not shake, the bed did not quiver or move, but suddenly, at the foot of my bed, suspended between the ceiling and bed, appeared *an angel*. There was no mysterious light, and she was not this snowy white that people talk about she was more natural, in ecru-colored robes which covered her feet, and she had beautiful wings at her shoulders, just like the feathers or wings of a big bird. She didn't speak or move, she just stood there at the foot of my bed. You notice that I keep saying *she*. Yes, it was a female *angel*, approximately thirteen or fourteen years old. How do I know? Well, you just know when it happens.

I've been so puzzled all these years, and I used to cry when I thought about her or talked about her. She has never been back, although I have prayed for her to come see me, tell me why she came, why me, why then? Will I ever see her again? How I love the memory and wish I could answer some questions! I have one theory, but in repeating it I risk being thought of as "a fanatical, doting mother." But I believe this appearance was related to my son's birth. He was born on his father's birthday thirty-eight years ago. His birth on that day was the happiest day of my life, and the child that he was, and the man that he has become, is as near to an *earth saint* as I could ever dream of. A person like him inside and out, as a father, husband, friend, man of his word, in the church and community and life in general could only happen to someone by the *grace from above*.

I'll always wonder, "Was this the message she carried?"

(For those)
Who say, "Our Lord is God,"
  and
Stand straight and steadfast,
The angels descend
(From time to time):
"Fear ye not!" they say,
"Nor grieve! But receive
The Glad Tidings . . ."

                    Koran
                  —s. xli. 30

•   •   •   •

You know, you can't pray for an angel to come, you can't request one, you can't buy one. *I believe it is only by grace from above that one could be sent to someone on earth,* and I know I will always wonder, why me, and will she ever come again?

I wish I could have told this story to you in person, how I see her now, how she hovered, suspended in my house, for me, at my feet. It was just so sweet, and may not sound on paper as it would in person.

Most sincerely,

Frances L. Lyles
Houston, Texas

*At the round earth's imagined
   corners blow
Your trumpets, angels . . .*
—JOHN DONNE
Holy Sonnets

• • • •

• • • • • • • • • • • • • • • • • • •

o few people are actually aware of angelic presence, and the ones who are have no one to converse with. This causes feelings of doubt and, even worse, freak-ishness. I know, I have been dealing with this situation since I was six years old.

Reading about others' encounters made me realize that freakish as it may seem, my encounter was a visual gift

Gustave Doré. Agony in the
Garden (detail).

given to a minority of people, and instead of keeping it quiet, it should be told to others.

My story:

When I was six years old, my parents decided to take a family vacation at a beach cabin for a few days. The first afternoon there was a typical one—swimming in the water, filtering the sand through our toes, baking in the sun, and cooking on the grill. I remember nothing unusual.

My brother and I were put to bed that night, and I remember having a difficult time falling asleep. I remember my brother was lying catty-corner to myself. The cabin bedroom had an A-pitched roof with a small window at the top covered with discolored plastic.

During the middle of the night I was awakened, not by a sound or a movement; I just opened my eyes, and when I did, I found my heart pounding so hard and so fast that my hands on my chest were moving with its rapid beats. I remember feeling my heartbeat in my throat and fear flushing through my body. Six angels surrounded my bed, three angels on my right and three angels on my left. Their bodies were shoulder to shoulder, no definite space separating them. They were quite tall and wide. I can't say that they were taller than an adult, though to my child's eyes they seemed huge.

Their radiant glow brightened the room, a very soft glow. I was able to see through them to see my brother sleeping, unaware of their presence. They all looked the same, each clothed in a light blue gown, free flowing. Their golden wings were intricate in design, somewhat bulky, in a closed position. Their faces were snow white, with small noses and light eyes. Their hair was golden, long and wavy. On the top of their heads were the famous halos, round, bright, and a little bit smaller than the diameter of their heads. Their hands were held together in a praying fashion. The angels were doing nothing, just staring back at me.

I tried opening and closing my eyes, over and over and over again. I thought if I closed my eyes long enough, they would think I was sleeping and leave. My body started to perspire with nervousness, realizing how delicate every moment was. I felt as if they were there to take me away, and I didn't want to leave my mother. I made sure my hands didn't leave my chest. I knew it was forbidden to touch them or even to try.

I have no idea how much time passed. It seemed as if we were watching each other for several minutes. Nothing happened. I closed my eyes for the last time and went to sleep.

When I opened my eyes, I was ecstatic to find the sun shining and Mom in the kitchen. I quickly went to her and told her about the angels. Mom, having been in a convent as a teenager, understood—but never explained.

Throughout the remainder of my childhood and my

"Truly, truly, I say to you, you will see heaven opened, and the angels of God ascending and descending upon the Son of Man."

—JOHN 1:51

• • • •

Everyone, no matter how humble he may be, has angels to watch over him. They are heavenly, pure and splendid, and yet they have been given us to keep us company on our way: they have been given the task of keeping careful watch over you, so that you do not become separated from Christ, their Lord.

And not only do they want to protect you from the dangers which waylay you throughout your journey: they are actually by your side, helping your soul as you strive to go ever higher in your union with God through Christ.

—POPE PIUS XII

• • • •

teenage years I often recollected that night, each time feeling a shiver of energy throughout my body. My eyes tear up. I have shared the story with only a chosen few, no one has ever understood or explained—how could they?

Sometimes I wonder why they came, for it just seems like nothing happened that night other than glancing at one another. I know we didn't exchange words. But sometimes it feels as if they granted me a gift that was to be realized in my later years.

Some people are gifted with angels saving their lives in dangerous instances; there are angels that speak wisdom to people and there are angels that bring gifts for the sake of mankind. I believe my encounter happened so that I could guide people in their faith and spiritual growth, as a teacher and healer.

So, to end, let's focus not on the why but just on the gift of vision and share the praise with others.

Dani R. Abel
Santa Ana, California

• • • • • • • • • • • • • • • • • •

y name is Denise Sexton. I'm twelve years old. Ever since I read *A Book of Angels*, I've been wanting to share these experiences with you.

When I was about nine, my aunt was murdered. I knew before anyone else. When I was playing, all of a sudden this warm breeze swept over me, and I felt that something was wrong. Two hours later I heard my parents saying that she had been killed.

A few days later I dreamed of seeing my aunt with the biggest, purest, clearest blue eyes I've ever seen. They seemed not to blink. I remember running, and when I looked back, I saw her with the most beautiful light I had ever seen! I really cannot explain it, but what stood out most were her eyes. And I am still in awe, for my mother says your eyes are the window to your soul.

A few days after that I had another dream. My aunt was lying beside me in my bed. She said she could stay for one night, that God had given her permission. She spoke in a soft, sweet voice that "filled" my body. Before she left, she told me that she had stayed in Purgatory for three days and to be as good as I could, for three days was a very long time and Purgatory was far worse than earth. When she left me, in her spot was a softly glowing

Ad Astra. 19th-Century
book plate.

light that kept me warm like a fire, even though we had
no heaters or such in our home.

Then in 1989, my seventeen-year-old brother died
from a blood clot. I can remember every part of him—

the way his fingernails were shaped and where his hair parted. We were very close, and I loved Darrell very much.

The night he died, I was staying at a friend's house. We were sitting on the waterbed when I felt the urge to look at my wrist where I was wearing a bracelet that was supposed to be for Darrell. Then I looked at the clock. It was 11:42 P.M. I then felt the bracelet break. Later I prayed and thanked God for Darrell and for making him happy, instead of asking for him to be well.

A few days later I was told that Darrell died at 11:42 P.M.

My most recent experience was a few weeks ago. I was in trouble and ran outside and leaned on the left side of my house, crying. There was no wind blowing, but it was cold. I looked toward the west, and all of a sudden I felt the softest breeze sweep over me. It was warm as if the sun were shining. I felt as though I was floating, but I could still feel my hands on the house. It seemed as if my tears were "blown" off my face, and a terrific *peace* settled over me.

Then I was back in my body and was being called inside, but that feeling of peace stayed with me the whole day.

Denise Sexton
Sebastopol, California

• • • • • • • • • • • • • • • • • •

nce in my bedroom I looked up, thinking I heard my husband's step, and saw an angel. He was very, very tall, and his head was going through the ceiling, which wasn't there anymore. The incredible thing was I knew him and he knew me. He held out his hand. "Come," he said. "I want to show you something."

I took his hand, unafraid, and then we were moving upward very fast.

He said, "Look." I looked and saw our earth spinning around itself while it was orbiting another path. It was so beautiful.

He said, "Look better," and I seemed to adjust my focus, like a camera, and saw a woman on the earth coming out of a grocery store, carrying a bag. I could even see freckles on her nose. It was glorious, and I was feeling so *good*!

He said, "Look even better," and then I saw that everything had sound and that all created things had a voice, little rocks had little voices, big rocks and mountains had big voices. They were all singing and praising; little stones in driveways were singing, and furniture and grass. The sea and the waves were all bringing their joy to the shores. I could hear them rushing to the beaches saying, "Halle—lu—iaaahhhhhh."

These sounds were so perfect and clean, it made me cry. My whole being wanted to cry. The trees and bushes didn't have leaves but little hands and they were clapping in abandon.

I said to the angel, "Oh, I'll never forget this."

He said, "See that you don't. All these things were created to praise and show God's glory, that is all they do. But man is created with a will, and he can't praise God unless he submits his will out of love for God. When he does this, God commands them to be silent because His child is praising Him."

He said, "When we don't praise God, the very rocks cry out."

And then I was back in my bedroom, reading the book of Isaiah, but I knew that what we see every day is not really what is there; instead all of it is held together by little singing, praising molecules of joy.

Anna Loomis

Corning, New York

It is only with the heart that one can see rightly; what is essential is invisible to the eye.
—ANTOINE DE SAINT-EXUPERY
The Little Prince

• • • •

Angel. Romanesque bas relief (detail). (ArchiPhoto)

n February 1987 I was at a retreat led by Jesuit priests, in an Anglican convent in Toronto, Ontario. Each person was appointed a director, who assigned Bible passages to read and "pray." I was told not to do the "required" assignments but to rest, sleep, and walk for the first two days—then to meditate and pray once a day only until I appeared less exhausted. I had recently separated from my husband of forty-one years and was in a demanding, fascinating job.

On the third day I sat in semiprayer/silence, and a picture appeared in front of me. Framed. A pathway stretched to a gateway with a cross partially showing. A white (female?) figure stood there, and all around angels floated, some with wings outstretched, others folded—many of them flying, suspended, watching. At the bottom was a Bible verse (and I am not good at quoting Bible verses):

> I will give mine angels charge over thee lest thou dash thy foot against a stone.

I think it's from Psalm 91. I watched for a while—then it faded as I started *thinking*.

To the heavenly angels, who possess God in humility and serve Him in blessedness, all material nature and all rational life are subject.

—SAINT AUGUSTINE

A few days later (Sunday night) I returned home and to work, only to be taken ill with what I thought was gastric flu. By Thursday I felt marginally better, temperature down some, and pain decreased. Before returning to work I checked in with my doctor, who ordered an ultrasound exam. The technicians running the scanner over my belly remarked, "Oh, look, the rock of Gibraltar," but would not answer my queries. Two hours later I was on the operating table with a perforated gallbladder and rocklike formation therein. The surgeons were puzzled at my rapid recovery and expressed their grave concern at my earlier danger! Little did they know the angels had been pressed into service—and indeed it was only a couple of weeks later that I remembered my angel vision and *most* appropriate verse, and I confess to chuckling at God's blessed sense of humor.

I know that when I often work with my hands, it is the healing guidance of the divine, manifest through my angels and those of the person with whom I work, that ensures safety and whatever good is accomplished. Sometimes I sense their presence and am thankful.

Muriel N. Bishop
Wallingford, Pennsylvania

• • • • • • • • • • • • • • • • • •

he first experience I would like to relate occurred when I was about nineteen or twenty. A group of friends went with me to a movie about Christ, and when I saw the scene of the Cross, it deeply troubled me. I decided to go home and talk to God about my feelings, for I was in tears and could not stop crying.

When I got home, I sat on my bed in the dark and just wept, thinking to myself and also to God that Jesus had given up His life so that mankind could believe in Him and experience peace and rest in this life. He had done everything He could, yet here was I, just as ignorant as when I had realized there was a God, just as blind and unknowing of Him as before I had agreed to follow His ways. What could Jesus do, more than He already had, to enlighten this ignorance of mine?!

I could feel within my being that comfort was trying to come to me, but I purposely refused it, because I wanted to hear from God Himself! After an hour or so (I really don't know just how long), I heard a voice, as plain as if someone were in the room with me, saying, "Go down and comfort her, for she weeps and she will not be comforted."

Immediately I felt a "lightening" presence in the room, and I looked up to see an angel descending into my

William Blake. Infant Angel.

room. He came through the ceiling as if there wasn't one there, and pausing for just a second at the foot of my bed, he looked at me as if trying to discern what the problem was. I say "he," but really it looked like a cross between male and female—not in body as much as in presence and character.

He was about five feet seven inches tall, both body and garments were pure white, and his hair was "well-set"—which is to say having loose curls all about his head, just long enough to cover his ears and the middle of his neck. I didn't know it then, but the overall look of this angel was similar to the Greek statues I have seen since that time. He was full in body and face, but not exceedingly muscular; he was certainly not made of skin and bone, however, and what would be the fleshy parts, such as the cheeks, arms, and calves of the legs, appeared quite soft, yet firm.

He came around to the side of the bed and sat beside me (his weight made the bed sink so that I was almost leaning into him); he put his right arm across my shoulders and his left hand on my left arm and, staring into my face, spoke quietly and yet firmly: "Why are you crying?"

For just a few seconds I found myself pausing to examine his eyes, which were white, and yet when I looked at them, I seemed to be able to see the universe; as if he were a vast portion of space fitted into a bodily form.

Therefore, with Angels and Archangels, and with all the company of heaven, we laud and magnify thy glorious Name; evermore praising thee, and saying,

Holy, Holy, Holy, Lord God of Hosts,

Heaven and earth are full of thy glory:

Glory be to Thee, O Lord Most High.

—Book of Common Prayer, SERVICE OF HOLY COMMUNION

• • • •

Ye who believe!
Celebrate the praises of God,

And glorify Him
Morning and night.

He it is Who sends
Blessings on you, as do
His angels, that He may
Bring you . . . into Light . . .
Koran
—s. *xxxiii. 41–43*

· · · ·

Finally, coming to my "senses," I proceeded to tell him exactly what I have expressed in this letter, about my ignorance and stupidity in the face of all that Christ had done so that men might change.

The angel looked intently at me, with great care, but with absolutely nothing that would inspire self-pity, and said directly, "Jesus died for you, too." I had no idea why that statement would do anything to help me, since I thought I already knew that, but as he was speaking, I "saw" (again within myself somehow) a "vision" (or whatever you wish to call it) of the universe, and from some high place there streaked a falling star. For a few seconds I watched as it descended like lightning into my own spirit, and when it hit the bottom of my soul, it exploded in a great pacific explosion of white light, which immediately gave peace to my being.

I saw also the scene of the Cross, and this time I saw Jesus, and as if I were looking through His eyes, I had a vision of what He was beholding at the time of His death. In it He saw me. Before, this knowledge had been somehow distant, but it now became very personal. I had known this, but I had not identified personally with it; and therefore it had not been able to minister to my spirit and give me the peace that I needed. Instead of being a troubled and horrible scene, the crucifixion now became a scene of great love and care.

Like a tap shutting off, my tears ceased. I was not troubled anymore. I was almost shocked at how released I felt in a split second of time, and I sat there, rather dumbfounded, looking at the angel, who was looking intently back at me. I expected him to get up and go back immediately, since I had the peace I had been seeking, but he sat there, looking at me, as if he were searching to see if there were anything else that I might bring up. I became embarrassed by this attention, and all I could do was smile and bow my head. He then got up and walked around to the foot of the bed, where he'd come in, and looked up in a most loving and worshipful manner, as if he were seeing God. A column of white light descended on him, and he rose through the ceiling, out of sight.

The "personableness" of this angel impressed me. People who like to think that progressing in spiritual life means making God more distant, intellectual, and almost characterless have missed the mark. He is the one who created personalities and characters, and He loves what He has created. He is not looking to "mature" us right out of the expression He made for us to live and move in.

The next experience I wish to relate occurred about five years later. I was working as a waitress in a hotel in town. I could hardly stand the place. I felt degraded, trapped, and broken, and this one morning while I was in the kitchen before work, my mother saw what she thought was a moth on the lampshade in the utility room. She called to see if I could get it outside.

The same Lord is Lord of all and bestows his riches upon all who call upon him.

—ROMANS 10:12

• • • •

First I turned the light off, and almost immediately this "moth" flew over to the wall, quite high. I was wondering how to get it down, when I felt an urge to put my hand next to the wall about six inches below the "moth." Then I heard something within my being speak, telling the thing to land on my hand.

No more than two or three seconds went by, and this "moth" pushed off from the wall and fluttered to my hand. I saw it was a butterfly, with a deep reddish-brown coat, yellow trim, and royal-blue spots on the corners of the wings. It didn't move. I walked around with it, and it stayed, sunning itself on my hand. I "wished it" to hop to my other hand, and it did. I held it toward a leaf on a tree and told it to hop to that leaf, and it did. Then, to make sure this was no "accident," I told it to hop back from the leaf to my hand—and it did.

By this time I realized God was giving me a message, and I called my mother to show her this event. She couldn't explain it either, but just watched this butterfly hopping from my hand to the tree several times. Finally I could feel that a message had gotten through to my spirit, and I let it hop onto a leaf one last time and fly away.

Later I looked up this butterfly and found it was called Mourning Cloak, a perfect simile for the period I was passing through; for just as the butterfly must end its life as a "worm" in order to emerge as a butterfly, so also I

Son, you are always with me,
and all that is mine is yours.
—LUKE 15:31

. . . .

Angel of the Annunciation.

was being asked to let the time of suffering and mourning pass through me and do its full work in order to emerge with a broader horizon.

There is a secret to having life's problems create a "change for the better" within you, instead of having them sap your strength. At the moment when a trial or insufferable situation is overtaking you, you must look to God with love and appreciation and let go of your own purpose and let God's love fill your inner being. You must embrace the "death" in order to obtain the life.

Brenda Brown
Cranbrook, British Columbia

. . . .

any years ago when our third son, Erich, was small, he relayed to me this story about his ceiling light. While he slept, it seems, his ceiling fixture loosed itself from its moorings, then descended, hovering and shimmering brilliantly over his body as he lay in bed. I knew this child to be highly intuitive, wiser than his years. He wasn't likely to feed me a line, tell me a lie— still, I reasoned, even Edison's best cannot come alive, does not move at will. "Maybe it wasn't your light coming down at all, but rather you going up," I said. But no, he had never left his bed, was wide awake, and it was the light—to these facts he stubbornly held fast.

The following night I was roused from a deep sleep by an insistent voice urging, "Wake up. Wake up! If you want to see Erich's light, it's right here in your room."

A brilliance, radiant, scintillating, shaped like a gigantic snowflake, lingered at my doorway. I felt a presence, an aliveness. It was warm, peaceful, good. As I watched, it began slowly to retreat, then fade, then was gone. I noted the time, determined to prove I was not asleep, and ever so slowly came to the realization that I, no more than my ten-year-old, could not put a name to this wondrous thing. Was it an angel in its natural state, not artificially clothed in human disguise? Could we be so happily blessed? Perhaps yes.

Best wishes,

Carole J. Hessner
Delavan, Wisconsin

. . . .

Fear Not: for, behold, I bring you good tidings of great joy.
—Luke 2:10

. . . .

At a certain point the appearance of the angel is no longer the important fact; rather it is the message that it brings. Is there a distinction? The messenger is the message in a way. "That's all an angel is," wrote the mystic Meister Eckhardt, "an idea of God."

The next letters describe epiphanies and revelations of God. These true mystical unions with the divine are not expressed through beings or spirits or even angels (although they, too, may be part of the vision), but through ecstasy, rapture, and light.

'm not even halfway through *A Book of Angels*, yet I feel compelled to write to you. I think the book serves as a confirmation for thousands of us who have had special experiences.

My story goes likes this:

My parents were good people but not particularly religious. My aunt and uncle, however, were quite devout. One Saturday evening they convinced my parents to let them take me to something called Youth for Christ. (I was about ten years old at the time.) My mother and father reluctantly agreed. Toward the end of the service those who hadn't been "saved" were encouraged to come forward. I was sitting between my aunt and uncle but I was promptly lifted out of my seat and pushed into the long, sloping aisle that led down to the pulpit. It was as if a strong force of air carried me along. My relatives were very upset, afraid of what my parents would think, afraid that they might be blamed for my actions.

That night as I slept there came a glorious, luminous burst of blinding light—I saw and sensed a few strokes of wings. I felt completely encompassed in light and overwhelming love. The next day people commented on my skin; it seemed to glow. My mother was afraid I was ill, but I was happier that day than I have ever been since.

If a person is seeking God, his Beloved is seeking him much more. . . . and the desire for God is the preparation for union with Him.

—St. John of the Cross
The Living Flame of Love

· · · ·

OPPOSITE: Botticelli.
Angels of the Nativity.

This hasn't been my only experience with divine intervention, but it is the most profound and lasting. I've always felt so fortunate because I needn't have blind faith. Because of my experience I *know* God exists. If something should cut short my life, I truly won't be afraid—because I have been visited by angels.

Jeanne Van Dusen Smith
Alexandria, Virginia

. . . .

n the night of August 26, 1989, I was putting clothespins in a bag that hung on the windowsill when I looked up and found myself standing face-to-face with the purest, brightest light I have ever seen in my entire life. It was as white as snow with a sparkle of what appeared to be mercury riding in the center. Although it stood motionless, I sensed a forceful and powerful energy. I knew right away it wasn't a car light because it looked solid and I felt a human presence, a thinking, feeling being. The light actually stared at me, getting my attention just the way a person gets your attention by staring at you so that you feel his energy and look up.

I froze in my tracks totally astonished to the point of not breathing, moving, or speaking. This all-pervasive light just appeared out of nowhere without sound or warning. When I looked up, there it was in all its glory, as if a piece of the moon came down to my window. I was stunned out of my wits because it just watched me. I looked at this miraculous light, and it was like finding a pool of cool water in a desert and hoping it wouldn't disappear before kneeling down to quench my thirst.

I stared at the light; my mind was trying to interpret this strange thing. The light just stood there about two inches from me, and the only thing separating us was the window screen. The light blocked off everything behind it and stood as motionless as the sun, but I felt that its potential brightness could have been ten times brighter than the sun. I thought that this light was restraining an explosive force to protect me from harm. I felt love generating from that light, and I felt very special that something so magnificent thought of my well-being.

I thought to myself that this could be God almighty or an angel of the Lord, but why on earth would God appear to me? Vanity began to play in my thoughts. My hair was in rollers and I didn't even have my makeup on. The big curlers made funny shapes in the scarf that was tied around my head.

I looked from the left to the right of it, and then I fastened my eyes on the middle as if looking for a center

Almighty God, unto whom all hearts are open, all desires known, and from whom no secrets are hid; Cleanse the thoughts of our hearts by the inspiration of thy Holy Spirit, that we may perfectly love thee, and worthily magnify thy holy Name; Amen.
—Book of Common Prayer

• • • •

of communication. During this whole time we just stared at each other, me in total amazement. It was like a hypnotic state where I couldn't move or make my brain waves decipher the message fast enough. I was about to commune with this glorious, wonderful white light, when my mind provided me with a message: the wrong message. My mind went from God to Unidentified Flying Object, and I started backing away from it.

As I did, the light moved sideways. I kept backing into the kitchen in a hypnotic daze, and my mother, who was sitting on the back porch, noticed the light. She said it lit up the whole back porch like lightning, and she also felt a human presence. She said when the light moved to the end of our house, it disappeared.

My nephew walked into the kitchen to the refrigerator. When he turned around, he said he saw what he thought was lightning that lit up not only the whole back porch but the kitchen and dining room as well. But there was no lightning or storm that night.

I documented every piece of information and for days kept thinking if I had left anything out. I called the air force and the National Aeronautics and Space Administration trying to find out if anyone else had reported this light. Then my mind began to wonder, why, out of all the people in the world, did this light appear to me? I began to feel that this was no accident.

Finally one day I remembered something that could

have set off the visitation. About two weeks earlier I was reading a Bible story, although I can't remember what it was about. I do know that Jesus performed a great miracle and I was in awe about it. I said to myself, "Why doesn't Jesus appear to us like that?"

Jesus must have wanted me to know that He is just as real today as He was back then. Maybe He saw my great faith in Him and wanted to reassure me that He is with us always.

Who knows, maybe during the short time I looked at the light, I did commune with God. I know from what I saw that He is kind and loving. He is pure and still as a calm and peaceful lake. He is marvelous and exciting, and I felt His suppressed energy. It's the kind of energy that could explode like a nuclear bomb, or softly caress a new-born.

I later read in the Bible that God is light. Nothing else could convince me more. God touched my life after the miraculous visitation. Maybe not right away, because I was uncertain of what I saw, but each day I am more and more convicted by my actions.

I want to be ready to commune with that beautiful light, to be a part of the new kingdom and walk with God in eternal peace.

Joyce Robinson-Brim
Washington, D.C.

• • • • • • • • • • • • • • • • • • •

Gustave Doré. Angel in the Garden of Eden.

have had several experiences. Here are three.

· THE WHITE DOOR AND FRAME ·

When I was about eight years old, I saw something I've never forgotten. We lived in the country. I was walking back toward our house, but was still midway in the pasture.

I felt inclined to look up toward the right, and I saw the most beautiful white door and its frame against a background of the most intense red clouds. I have never seen a red like it again. It was very vaporous-looking and very beautiful. What it meant I do not know. I just remember it. It was my first experience of something I could not explain.

· THE HOLDING-HAND EXPERIENCE ·

I had been going through a rather difficult time in the mid eighties. I had a teenage daughter who was trying to do her own thing, and my health was not good.

One night as I went to bed, I said my prayers and was nearly asleep. I was physically very tired and really wanting sleep. All of a sudden I heard this voice say to me, "I want to hold your hand." For whatever reason I was not frightened, but very calm and very sleepy. As I was lying on my right side, I offered my left hand. "No," the voice gently said, "I want to hold your right hand." So I offered my right hand and then instantly fell asleep. The next morning I remembered what had happened and wondered about it. A few days later a friend gave me a book on Bible promises. For about a week I had no time to pick up the book. Then one day I did—and on the page I opened it to, I read, "I will hold your right hand and I will comfort you. Be not afraid."

Well, I was filled with humility and love, realizing that God had come to comfort me in a very real way.

He shall cover thee with his feathers, and under his wings shalt thou trust: his truth shall be thy shield and buckler.

—Psalm 91: 4

• • • •

· THE RAPTURE ·

Human words will not be able to express the feelings of this experience, but I will do the best I can.

In 1980 (I am forty-eight) I began to be ill. I was always tired, with muscle weakness and severe bone pain. I kept putting off going to the doctor. My grown children were on my case to seek medical attention. I was really afraid I had cancer of the spine and finally went to the Ochner Foundation in New Orleans. I was diagnosed as having an autoimmune disease. It's very much like M.S. I was disturbed because I knew no insurance company would insure me. I asked the doctor if the tests could be wrong.

And what doth the Lord require of thee, but to do justly, and to love mercy, and to walk humbly with thy God?

—Micah 6:8

• • • •

He said that I did not think so, but that there was another battery of tests I could take. They would be very costly. I told him I would think about it for a few days and get in touch with him when I had decided what I wanted to do.

I went home and for the next three days I prayed to God. I was troubled. On the third day, after tending to my household chores, I went into the bathroom to take a shower. I had just begun bathing when all of a sudden I felt a presence there with me. I always understood that this presence was Jesus. I became enraptured, totally absorbed, no longer aware of my surroundings. He told me that yes, I did have the disease that had been diagnosed, but not to fear, that it would never be too bad for me. (This disease is sometimes fatal, and the sufferings are great.) For the past three days I had thought of nothing else, but now I no longer cared whatsoever. All I cared about was what I was experiencing. I felt an unearthly love and feelings of security I could never, ever have believed possible. No words could convey these feelings. They were not of this world. But now I know they exist. If this presence would have said to me, "Come now, I will take you to where I am going," I would have dropped everything to go with Him. I wish I could do this experience justice in its retelling, but I cannot. Needless to say, it changed my life. I know for myself "God is, God loves, God cares." I am no longer afraid to die. While I love my life, I will never again fear losing it. Wonders await us we can't begin to imagine.

Alice Guidry
Thiboudaux, Louisiana

• •

his is an "epiphany" I had when I was about five years old. One warm spring day on our farm near Jerome, Idaho, I was quietly sitting alone on an old poplar-tree log. Mom used the log to kill and dress chickens on, so there were quite a few feathers around. Nearby was a badly weathered chicken house. To my amazement everything took on a profound glimmering. I had an expanded sense of understanding everything before my eyes. The weathered wood of the chicken house looked supernatural and seemed to be sort of divine. Even the feathers seemed to have a divinity in them. I felt a tremendous inner peace and knowingness, far beyond anything my five-year-old vocabulary could get out. It seemed as if I could understand at a molecular level and that everything before me was good. The next two or three days after this experience it was cold and windy, and I repeatedly

Happy those early days, when I
Shined in my angel-infancy!
Before I understood this place
Appointed for my second race.
*—*HENRY VAUGHN
The Night

• • • •

sat on the log trying to get that something back, but nothing happened. To this day the memory stands out as an experience I would pay handsomely to have again.

Jack Kleinkopf
Shelton, Washington

. . . .

I live and love in God's peculiar light.
—MICHELANGELO BUONAROTTI
"Sonnet"

. . . .

just bought your book on angels today and saw the note about mystical experiences that you are collecting. I thought I would send along an account of one I had several years ago. I am sending a photocopy of the journal entry recounting it.

I wanted to clarify the mantra I was using during the experience. Most religious Jews are very careful about how they write any name of G-d or even the word itself, and, as you notice, even in English I leave out the vowels. That is to prevent any desecration of the name.

I am not an Orthodox Jew. I am sort of traditional and belong to a Reform and also a Reconstructionist synagogue. I am just an ordinary person in all respects.

This experience has stayed with me and it remains a jewel of mine, secreted away. I have told only two other people about it. I would prefer that my name not be used. Good luck with your endeavors.

MAY 9, 1988

Last night I had a strange and wonderful experience. I'm not sure what to think of it. I will just wait and see how it affects my life. I was working on the meditation course and was reading until fairly late. When I went to bed I was quite tired but I woke up a short time later and couldn't get back to sleep. I seemed to be half asleep but also filled with some sort of tension or urgency. I got up, and the feeling—quite physical—did not go away. I decided to try some relaxation. I usually don't meditate in the middle of the night. However, the desire was so strong that as soon as I sat and tried relaxation I felt more comfortable. Still, the urge to let go and let myself drift deeper into meditation was very strong. It was as if something outside or inside myself was taking over. So I let it. It was as if G-d Himself wanted to talk to me. I went quite deep fast, and indeed my body wasn't my own anymore.

The feeling of love and devotion pervaded me, and my mind repeated over and over as a mantra the words, *Adonai Elohai*, which is Hebrew for "Oh, L-rd, my G-d." It is difficult to describe how I felt. It was like being totally in love. I wanted only to go deeper and deeper, be totally lost in G-d. I begged Him to let me come to Him

*Learn, too, how God's own
   angels keep
Your ways by day, your dreams
   asleep.*
—NORREYS JEPHSON O'CONOR
   "To a Child"

• • • •

only, forever. My arms, not of my own volition, opened out and upward as if to embrace Him. Then, later, I felt as if my heart were being removed and a sign placed on it. The sign was the four-letter Hebrew tetragrammaton which is read right to left, "Adonai," or L-rd. But the letters were placed one on top of the other, not horizontally, so you couldn't distinguish each one exactly. And then my hands lifted some more, and I felt so much love in each one that it was tangible.

I was repeating the mantra in my head and telling G-d that I would do as He pleased and I was His to do with as He pleased, whatever—even if it was hard for me, even if it meant staying here—as I had begged Him to take me to Him. I could have stayed that way forever. I thought about whether this experience would change me, if by looking at me people would know that His name was written on my heart as it is on the angels' hearts. After that my hands came together over my chest—again by themselves—and when they touched, it was as if they didn't belong to me. Some short time later they came over my face, and it was as if my face were being caressed by someone who loved me very much. It was so beautiful. Toward the end I rocked a bit back and forth in love and ecstasy. After another short time the kitchen timer went off (for some reason), and I felt as if there were a rose being given me, and I would not have been surprised to find a single rose lying on the bed. I lay down and felt again not a part of myself but also not in a trance either—or not the same as before. I felt like a Buddha (a reclining Buddha that I've seen in the pictures)—here but not here either. And I fell asleep.

This whole incident was mediated by angels—two beings whom I really did not see, but felt. When they were done, they asked if I wanted to come back, and I agreed.

It is morning, and I still feel pervaded by love. I wondered how what I have been reading and my thoughts about meditation class have influenced this experience.

My one thought from last week was that the best requisite for a mystical life is to have both feet planted firmly on this earth in the physical.

Name withheld by request

. . . .

Angels of the Nativity.

've discovered that I have many spiritual guides who have helped me over the years, but I was not aware of them until July 1985.

In 1985 I was thirty-three years old, living in upstate New York, and working as an elementary school teacher. I had just ended a very long, intense, intimate relationship, and I was emotionally traumatized. Deeply depressed, I was forced to quit my job. I considered suicide but somehow knew inside my heart that I did not have the courage to do it. I ruled out alcohol and drugs as temporary escapes since I had always detested their use. Instead I suffered alone.

One very memorable night I was feeling so desperate I cried out loud for divine help. I distinctly remember being amazed with myself, because I was of the Hebrew faith, and I shouted aloud, "Jesus, you don't know me because I have never believed in you, but if you're really there, please help me!" At that point I was so emotionally drained and exhausted, I fell asleep. In the early hours of the morning I suddenly awoke and saw that the criss-crossing steel beams that supported my ceiling were glowing in the shape of a large cross. I sat up in bed to be certain I wasn't dreaming. I looked at my clock, which read 3:00 A.M. Then, quite clearly, I saw a golden light shimmering above my head and surrounding the large cross. I could not take my eyes off the cross and stared in complete amazement. The ceiling beams had been painted black, and since my curtains were pulled shut, I could not mistake the golden light for moonlight. Suddenly, as I sat transfixed, I heard a clear voice within my mind proclaim, "Fear Ye Not, I am the Lord." A warmth spread through my body, and I felt comforted and deeply peaceful. I lay back down in my bed and drifted back to sleep.

OPPOSITE: Matthias Grünewald. Angel Musicians.

And to God doth obeisance
All that is in the heavens
And on earth, whether
Moving creatures
Or the angels; for none
Are arrogant before their Lord.

—*s. xvi. 49*

• • • •

I can't describe the feeling of elation that came over me the next day as I looked around at the sky and earth with a new appreciation. Nature revealed itself as I've never seen it before. It seemed as though I had developed new senses; colors were so vivid! Joyously I kept gazing up toward the sky, overwhelmed with deep appreciation. I felt a deep longing to be up in the blue sky instead of on earth—so much so, I decided to go to my county airport for a ride in a single-engine plane that very day! As I flew with the pilot in a Cessna, I had a feeling of intense joy and déjà vu, as though I had done this many times before. I was so elated, the pilot encouraged me to take flying lessons.

After my "flight to the heavens" I began to have strong desires to help other people. I had a new sense of purpose and a need to help the elderly, the homeless, and prisoners—the "forgotten ones." I responded to an ad for a summer position teaching in a New York State prison. For the rest of that summer I taught and counseled inmates, which turned out to be a very emotionally rewarding experience for me. I also visited nursing homes and found that I could give spiritual advice to the residents.

From September to December 1986 I began to receive messages from "beyond the third dimension." I saw apparitions and had incredible "past life" dreams. I contacted friends who had died and had many other psychic experiences in which I knew things about people I had just met. I also became blessed with the gift of automatic writing and transmitted messages from discarnates. Some, whom I have never met in their earthly lives, would deliver messages to others through me.

Of the many messages I received "from beyond," three were particularly amazing and significant. I communicated with three spirits known as Willy, John, and Steve. Incredibly, I discovered their former identities six months later when I met my new boyfriend! They had been his best friends and they had all been killed in Vietnam. We were stunned! My boyfriend accepted the messages I relayed to him from my new spirit friends. They asked him to stop blaming himself for their deaths (he had served in the air force in Vietnam with them) and informed him that there was really no such thing as death, merely a passage from one dimension to another.

Willy, in particular, has been a strong spiritual guide to us. His first message was, "Help will come at the Wall." At the time I had no idea what the message meant, and in fact, did not even know that my new boyfriend was a Vietnam vet, since we had just met. I did not make any connection until 1988, when we felt compelled to visit the Vietnam War memorial in Washington, D.C. My boyfriend had never been emotionally able to visit "the Wall" before. Messages from Willy became very strong, however, and we knew that we needed to go to Washington.

At the Wall there were so many names, we were over-

Oh, then, soul most beautiful among all the creatures, so anxious to know the dwelling place of your Beloved that you may go in quest of Him and be united with Him, now we are telling you that you yourself are his dwelling . . . his secret chamber and hiding place.
        —ST. JOHN OF THE CROSS
        The Spiritual Canticle

• • • •

whelmed. I had never been to the memorial before, but I heard Willy say "E Five and Seven." I repeated it aloud, while questioning what it could mean. We moved to the east side, but couldn't find any of the names we were looking for. I decided to go to the directory, while my boyfriend continued searching at the east end. I found Willy's name on the directory. His birth date was May 7, (fifth month, seventh day). The directory indicated E-13. I returned to the east side and told my boyfriend to look for Plaque 13. We were very surprised to find that he had been standing smack in front of it. Willy's name was on the twelfth line: E-5 + 7; 5 + 7 = 12!

I walked away so that my boyfriend could meditate and have whatever solitude he could find among the hundreds of people crowding around. I went back to the west side and had my own talks with Willy, my friend from the spirit world. Then I felt compelled to snap a picture of my boyfriend off in the distance, standing in front of Willy's name. I could hardly see him in the crowd, and I wondered why I felt so strongly about taking his picture, lost as he was among so many people. I thought a photo would barely show him in such a "mob."

We ended our visit to Washington and returned home. A week later I had my film developed and had quite a shock! The picture I had taken of my boyfriend standing in front of Willy's name at the Wall shows him standing alone! All the other people were quite far away, and he distinctly stands out, completely apart from them! My boyfriend exclaimed that he distinctly remembered being surrounded by throngs of people. He then told me that Willy had always known there was a side of him that would never believe things unless he had scientific proof. I had been trying to convince him that Willy's soul was still alive, that it hadn't died and was still communicating with him through the messages I was receiving. Amazed as he was at the information I had been receiving, he still had a hard time believing it. Now Willy had provided that final proof with the photograph!

Since that time I have received other messages from spirits existing at much higher vibratory levels. The messages are all the same. We are all one, and there is no such thing as death, merely a passing from one form to another. We are all sparks from the Creator, and our ultimate goal is to be perfected souls. The universe is far-reaching, beyond dimensions that we know here on earth, and we are never alone. There exist in every dimension "guides," whose purpose it is to help us advance spiritually toward a reunion with All That Is, the Universal Intelligence that created all energy. We are all one group mind that exists throughout the universe, which is filled with light and love. We are all connected.

Marcia Mitnick
Hudson, New York

"Hey, angel," Amarante called out in his dream. "What's a rainbow doing over our town on a sunny day like today?"

. . . "Maybe it's because for once in your lives you people are trying to do something right."

Abruptly the angel disappeared.

—JOHN NICHOLS
The Milagro Beanfield War

•   • • • • •

This beautiful account is the story of a mother dying of cancer who saw four angels at her bed, each holding one corner of the sheet. They promised—and gave—her more time to live. Interestingly the dog saw the angels, too.

 have never seen an angel, but my mother was visited by a group of them, and last November I wrote down every true word of it, her angel story. This is the first time I have submitted it to a stranger's eyes.

I read dozens of books after my mother's death to ease the pain. Yours was the only one that succeeded in doing so. This story is all I can do to repay you.

"Is there anything in particular you want to talk about?" my mother asked, but with a stranger's voice. Her throat was so raw from the tubes and machines, and her lungs so saturated with fluid, that even the simplest words were thickly coated with involuntary and sometimes almost unintelligible inflections.

It was a language I had learned to interpret these last few months, regretfully, bitterly. Still, I could not answer her question at first. I looked down at my hands clasped in my lap.

My mother smiled patiently, waiting for me to speak. Her face, stripped by cancer to its barest, fragile essence, was still beautiful. With her newly hairless, smooth head, she appeared at once impossibly old and impossibly young. But, like anything of great beauty, her face had become something I could not rest my eyes upon for longer than a few seconds without shrinking back from its intense power. I pressed my body deeper into the vinyl-cushioned side of the ambulance.

"No, Mom, nothing in particular," I answered with a sigh. Then I confessed, unable, as always, even as a teenager with the most urgent of motivations, to lie to her.

"Just everything, Mom. I just want to talk about everything."

Every big thing and every little thing that will happen to me for the rest of my life, I thought to myself. *I need all the answers to all the questions I would have asked you years before, if I had known to ask them. I want your advice on raising my daughter, your first granddaughter, who, now too young to know you, will have to borrow my memories, already darkened by the shadows of terminal disease. But most of all let's talk about how, exactly how, step by step, I am going to live the rest of my life without you—my one and only safe harbor of unconditional love.*

This is what I wanted to say, but remained silent instead. Spoken words could not do this moment justice, I painfully realized.

"I know," she said, in the saddest tone yet of that stranger's voice, as if she had just read my thoughts from the worried lines of my face.

I stared at her, momentarily shocked by the sudden change in her eyes. My mother's extraordinary ocean-blue eyes were now filled with the pale-yellow tears of any dying woman. When had this happened? Last night? Last minute, when my head was turned down? This was the ultimate deprivation, to be robbed of seeing her unique qualities, to see her only, and finally, in terms of dwindling bodily functions.

I glanced out of the rear windows of the ambulance, stroking the back of her limp hand in a slow, steady rhythm, trying to comfort myself as well as her by keeping contact when I could no longer look at her or speak to her.

She was breathing so shallowly, I concentrated upon her now-tiny body (tiny except for the huge, swollen abdomen) before I detected a slight, uneven movement of her swaddled form. I had stopped breathing myself as I death-watched her, utterly transfixed with terror.

I breathed out a desperate prayer: *Please God, wait until we get her home. Let it happen in her own bed, in peace.*

"The bottom line is that she has a tumor that is growing rapidly and will result in her death in the next twenty-four hours."

This is what her oncologist said to us late last night in the hospital corridor, his eyes dropping to the floor.

"It could be a particularly agonizing kind of death," he added, now speaking directly to our feet.

My sisters stood there with me, flanking our father. I clutched a notepad to my chest, where I had carefully written down all of our questions. Somehow we had figured that if we just asked this man the right question, he would finally give us the answer we hoped for. But now none of the questions about the quality of our mother's life mattered any more after being given the answer of death. Still, my father choked one out.

"Will she make it until we get her home?"

The doctor gave my father a look I had seen on his face once before. It was ten months earlier, when the diagnosis had been made, and after listening to his clinical speech my mother had asked him a single question. The room was so quiet, I remember thinking I actually heard the sound of our hearts breaking as she spoke.

Think nothing else but that God ordains all, and where there is no love, put love, and you will draw out love.

—St. John of the Cross
Letter to María de la Encarnación

• • • •

"Do I have one good year left?" she had asked.

And the doctor had answered my mother then with this same wary expression.

Unfortunately he had been right. It had not even been a year, and certainly not enough of what had occurred since then had been good.

My father flinched at the silent message on the doctor's face. And then he spoke in a voice I remembered from over twenty years before, an incredibly resonant, strong voice, the way as a child I had imagined God sounded.

"I have arranged for a private ambulance to take my wife home as soon as she wakes up tomorrow morning. I expect you to be there, and take every damn tube, and I mean every one, out of her so that she can go home the way she should—the way a person who is as loved and cherished as she is should."

"Yes of course," he said simply.

He was visibly relieved. There was nothing else for him to do, and best of all, nothing else he was expected to do. The passing of the torch, so to speak, for the home stretch.

"Have we gone over the bridge yet, darling?" my mother asked, waking surprisingly alert.

I looked out for a familiar landmark and saw that we were slowing down to glide through the sleepy Maryland eastern-shore town that my parents had retired to a couple of years earlier. I recognized a few of our neighbors outside their houses, standing in a solemn salute to the ambulance passing through, acknowledging its precious cargo.

They had been there for her, the way only a rural community still knows how to be. Leaving freshly baked, still-warm casseroles on the doorstep at five o'clock, weeding her flower garden when she was away for chemotherapy, clearing brush from the shoreline so that she could see the water from her bed. People made of solid gold.

"Mom, we're almost there, we're going through town."

The ambulance crept up our driveway, and I could see my father and sisters standing outside the front door, waiting. The sight of their wretched vigil struck me, and I burst into tears. So, this is how I must look, how we all look, the exposed faces of premature grief.

How terrible for her to remember us this way. How equally terrible for *us* to remember *her* this way. I threw myself angrily against the doors, just as they opened, and gasped the rain-filled air, as I scrambled out. I escaped, unnoticed, for all eyes and hands were on her now.

I have only the filmiest memories of those first hours of my mother's return. I do not remember exact words, or precise events, but at some remarkable point during the early evening, right before our eyes, she turned her

OPPOSITE:
Gustave Doré. Illustration from *The Divine Comedy*

own corner, one that no physician had foreseen or even held out the remotest possibility of existing. And the next morning she woke up, her abdomen completely flat, got out of bed, and made a pot of coffee for her incredulous family.

"There were four angels with me last night," she announced quietly, her soft voice restored.

My sisters and I smiled at the same time, each of us thinking that she was referring to her four daughters, because, angels or not, we had taken turns listening, every moment of the night, our ears pressed against a baby monitor, to the sounds of her continued breathing.

"No," she said, reading our thoughts, "four angels came in the night, and each held one corner of the sheet a few inches above my stomach."

She looked across the table solemnly at each of us in succession. My father looked down at his hands, but the rest of us held her gaze, steady, utterly believing.

"And, they are still waiting for me, but they said that I must have faith because there is still some time left. And I know what all the doctors have said, but you all must listen to me, because the angels told me. And so, let's make some plans, now."

And then she proceeded to give us her wish list. To pick up the new boat and go on a family ride across the creek. To have my daughter flown out to see her one more time. To arrange a small dinner party to thank her closest friends. Small wishes. Yet, the day before, they had been beyond our most far-reaching prayers.

My sisters began a grocery list in preparation for the dinner, and I followed my mother back into the bedroom.

"Mom," I started to say, not even knowing what my question was.

She adjusted her brightly colored silk scarf around her bare scalp, and looked up at me defiantly.

"Darling, it was not a dream. It was not even a vision. It happened, and *they* were here, as surely as you are standing here right now. And," she added, pointing to Danny, our aged golden retriever in his favorite position on the end of her bed, "*he* had to shove one of the angels aside last night before he could find a place to lie down. I watched him nudge an angel gently with his nose so that he could sleep here."

We both stared at the dog, who rolled his chestnut eyes toward me, tilting his head up proudly, as if he knew full well the importance of being sole witness to my mother's story.

"So, you see, you have time to fly back to California and bring my granddaughter here so that I can see her again."

I buried my face in the dog's neck, hiding my bewilderment, and listened blissfully to her plans for her short, but still existent future. I had always believed that if God had to choose one animal to enter heaven, it would be a golden retriever. My mother's revelation only strengthened my convictions.

"The angels told me that God has chosen my time," she said "but He is allowing me to choose the hour."

And so indeed He did. In the next few weeks she hosted her dinner party, although informally attired in her bedclothes, and she had Communion in her living room, the minister stepping good-naturedly over the sleeping dog on the floor so as not to spill the blessed wine. And she went out on the water for a short ride on a calm day in my father's new boat. And she saw my daughter once more and listened to her giggle abandonedly the way only a two-year-old, untouched by the closeness of death, can. And more small things, but enormous to us by the mere fact of their occurrence. Each one a gift, from God, through her, to us. The gift of answered prayers.

And then, six weeks later, my mother chose her hour. She was home, sleeping in her bed, holding my father's hand. I did not ask, but I am sure our God was somewhere nearby. And I am surer still, that even closer to her side were those special friends that only my mother and our dog had been granted the privilege to meet, returning once more to reclaim their precious charge.

Jacquelin A. Gorman
Manhattan Beach, California

• • • • • • • • • • • • • • • • • •

Angel of the Annunciation.

ftentimes after I've put my daughter to bed and done the dishes and picked up, I will look at the stars at night, just to unwind a little and to realize there really is a big world out there. Usually any prayers consist of "Thy will be done" or turning over any problems I may be clinging to and giving thanks. Or I may look out the window at the woods around my house to break away from my daily routine.

This particular day I had put my daughter to bed in the early evening. It was still light out. I walked into the other bedroom and knelt down by the window to look out at the woods, which I love. This is truly one of the strangest experiences I've had since becoming aware of a Higher Power. As I looked out the window (and I was not thinking about anything in particular), I felt as if every living item in the woods, particularly the leaves on the trees, all "breathed" in unison. At the same time there was an incredibly strong pull in my gut or stomach that moved (or breathed) in unison with the leaves, and it was involuntary on my part. It was like a surrender, as if a power much stronger than I flowed through me and nature at the exact same moment. We were unified, as if there was a purpose and meaning to every living thing. I felt so humbled, my head dropped down and I cried. It

Every breath of air and ray of light and heat, every beautiful prospect, is, as it were, the skirts of their garments, the waving of the robes of those whose faces see God.

—CARDINAL
JOHN HENRY NEWMAN

· · · ·

was a very beautiful, very humbling, very unusual experience for me. I don't know why or how this happened: It only made me realize the vast power and potential and purpose of all living things.

I can't say I would understand if someone described this to me. All I know is it happened, and I think we're all here for a purpose and God loves all His children.

Name withheld by request

. . . .

 *We come now to the end of these accounts, the fallen leaves drifting on the waters of our mind, the angels' letters that have come—and are gone as instantly—like whispers. Were they really there? How is it we have nothing now to show for them except a sense of grace, a fragile hope, the knowledge of our unity, and a sweet shiver passing over us, all because these letters, beckoning us to higher states, carry the signature of God?*

Angel letters.

Beckoning to more. To what?

In April 1990 I was interviewed on WOR-Radio in New

Life is like a path, and we all have to walk the path. If we lay down, we can lay down on that path. If we live through the night, we have to get up and start walking down that path again. As we walk down that path we'll find experiences like little scraps of paper in front of us along the way. We must pick up these pieces of scrap paper and put them in our pockets . . . Then, one day, we will have enough scraps of papers to put together and see what they say. Maybe we'll have enough to make some sense. . . . Read . . . then put the pieces back in that pocket and go on, because there will be more pieces to pick up. . . .

—UNCLE FRANK DAVIS:
Pawnee

. . . .

York by Gil Gross. He told the following story about a young couple who had one little girl and a new baby. The little girl wanted to be left alone with the baby, but the parents were afraid. They had heard of jealous children hitting new siblings, and they didn't want the baby hurt.

"No, no," they said. And, "Not yet."

And also: "Why do you want to be with him? What are you going to do?"

"Nothing. I just want to be alone with him."

She begged for days. She was so insistent that the parents finally agreed. There was an intercom in the baby's room. They decided that they could listen, and if the baby cried, if the little girl hit the baby, they could rush into the room and snatch the infant up. So, the little girl went in, approached the crib. Alone. She came up to the newborn baby, and over the intercom they heard her whisper, "Tell me about God. I'm forgetting."

OPPOSITE: Gustave Doré. Angel Appearing to Joshua.